IT Infrastructure Library

IT Infrastructure Library practices in small IT units

LONDON: HMSO

The Government Centre for Information Systems

Acknowledgements

Many people have contributed to this work. The following assistance is gratefully acknowledged.

Jennifer Ellwood-Wade of Bowood Systems Consulting, Auckland (under contract to CCTA), who did much of the initial planning work.

Tony Jenkins of Domain etc (under contract to CCTA), who carried out the analysis of ITIL roles.

Several CCTA customers commented on the draft versions, and contributed valuable ideas, especially:

Alan Dungavel and Boyd Glen of the Forestry Commission
Jim Nicol of the General Register Office (Scotland)
Ian Gray of the Overseas Development Administration.

Dorothy Graham of Grove Consultants and Paul Herzlich of Système Evolutif for ideas on introducing software tools.

Rob and Jenny Waller of the Information Design Unit (under contract to CCTA) who worked on the structure, tone and layout of the book.

© **Crown copyright 1995**

Applications for reproduction should be made to
HMSO Copyright Unit

First published 1995

ISBN 0 11 330674 1

For further information regarding CCTA products please contact:

CCTA Library
Rosebery Court
St Andrews Business Park
Norwich NR7 0HS

Contents

		Introduction	**7**
1		**Introduction to the IT Infrastructure Library (ITIL)**	**9**
	1.1	The ITIL approach	9
		1.1.1 Service support	10
		1.1.2 Service delivery	11
		1.1.3 The other ITIL sets	12
		1.1.4 Other ITIL services	13
	1.2	The focus of this text	13
2		**The significance of size**	**16**
	2.1	Defining small	16
		2.1.1 Absolute size	16
		2.2.2 Relative size	16
		2.1.3 Stability	17
	2.2	Characteristics of small and large IT units	17
		2.2.1 Informal culture	18
		2.2.2 Team spirit	19
		2.2.3 Quick communication	19
		2.2.4 Responsive	19
		2.2.5 Flexible	20
		2.2.6 Understanding of the business	20
		2.2.7 Relying on individuals	21
		2.2.8 Nowhere to hide	21
		2.2.9 Wide knowledge	22
		2.2.10 Limited knowledge	22
		2.2.11 High unit costs	23
		2.2.12 Per capita complexity	23
	2.3	Deciding on the size of an IT unit	24
	2.4	Scaling down for small IT units	25
3		**Establishing IT Service Management in small IT units**	**27**
	3.1	Setting the ITSM strategy	27
		3.1.1 A simple hierarchical view	27
		3.1.2 A more complex view	28
		3.1.3 Implications of the business strategy for ITSM	29
		3.1.4 Resourcing the ITSM strategy	30
	3.2	Developing the ITSM plan	30
		3.2.1 Identifying constraints	30
		3.2.2 Assigning priorities	31

	3.3	Agreeing and delivering the IT service		33
		3.3.1	Relationships with customers	33
		3.3.2	Documenting and supporting the service	34
		3.3.3	Relationships with suppliers	35
		3.3.4	Organising the unit to meet service goals	37
	3.4	Extending Service Management beyond IT		38
		3.4.1	Extending the Help Desk function	39
		3.4.2	Extending Service Level Management	40
	3.5	Using external skills		41
		3.5.1	Skills transfer	41
		3.5.2	Cross-servicing	42
		3.5.3	Recommendations for working with external suppliers	42
	3.6	Developing the service		43
	3.7	ITSM and the IT infrastructure		44

4 Managing a small IT unit — 45

	4.1	Adopting a hands-on approach		45
		4.1.1	Keeping time records	45
	4.2	Managing tasks		46
		4.2.1	Matching skills and tasks	46
	4.3	Managing the technology		47
		4.3.1	Single-source maintenance agreements	48
		4.3.2	Joint maintenance agreements	48
	4.4	Managing administration		48

5 Creating an organisational structure for ITSM in small IT units — 50

	5.1	Allocating tasks for ITSM		50
		5.1.1	Underlying Assumptions	53
	5.2	Scaling down ITSM roles for full-time staffing		54
	5.3	Adapting roles in-house		55
		5.3.1	Role 1: Problem and Availability Management	55
		5.3.2	Role 2: Help Desk	56
		5.3.3	Role 3: Configuration management, Change management and Software control and distribution	58
		5.3.4	Role 4: Costing and capacity management	59
		5.3.5	Role 5: Contingency Planning	60
		5.3.6	Role 6: Service Level management, Help Desk management, Charging	60

6	**Specialist software tools**			63
	6.1	Software tools for SITUs		63
		6.1.1	Service Support	63
		6.1.2	Service Delivery	64
		6.1.3	CAST – regression testing, documentation and repeatability	64
		6.1.4	Decision support software	65
	6.2	How to use tools successfully		65
		6.2.1	Justifying tools	68
	6.3	User guides		68
7	**Processes on the fringe of ITSM**			71
	7.1	System Security		72
		7.1.1	Security Risk Analysis	72
		7.1.2	Detecting Viruses	72
	7.2	Business Continuity Management		74
	7.3	Data management		75
	7.4	Software maintenance		76
	7.5	Testing and acceptance of hardware and software		76
		7.5.1	Business testing	77
		7.5.2	Spreadsheets and personal databases	78
8	**Measuring performance**			79
	8.1	Objectives and metrics		79
		8.1.1	External metrics	80
		8.1.2	Internal metrics	81
		8.1.3	Measuring customer perceptions	82
	8.2	Health checks and assessments		83
		8.2.1	Assessment of current performance	83
		8.2.2	Plan for improvement	83
		8.2.3	Implementing health checks	83
9	**Bibliography**			85
Annex A	Glossary			86
Annex B	IT Service Management – task allocation guide			88
Annex C	Where to go for advice			103
Annex D	Suggested contents for a user handbook			105
Annex E	Stable infrastructures within a small IT unit			109

Introduction

After five years of development, the IT Infrastructure Library (ITIL) reached completion in 1994. It documents best practice in IT Service Management (ITSM) in a consistent and integrated way. However, while ITIL was not specifically written for large-scale, data-centre-type operations, it was certainly written with such installations in mind, since they represent the traditional approach to IT within UK Government.

Now the success of ITIL means that it is being adopted by a vast range of IT units, covering all sizes, platforms and sectors. In fact ITIL has become the ITSM de-facto standard in many sectors and is fast becoming so in others. In many of these IT units, users have to adapt ITIL's general advice to their particular circumstances.

This book looks specifically at ITIL in small IT units (SITUs), focusing on the different nature of these environments and how ITIL techniques apply. However, some of the ideas it contains will be equally relevant to larger organisations.

In many such units, senior staff should, in theory, be familiar with guidance covering the whole range of IT provision and support. In practice, it would be impossible to know everything and still find time to run the unit. So much guidance is forced into the category of Defensive Shelfware – there just isn't time to read it all, but at least it is there to turn to in case of trouble.

This book is designed to be both short enough for busy people to read, and also useful enough to encourage small IT units to adapt and adopt appropriate ITIL ideas. It isn't comprehensive, so where appropriate, we refer to other guidance (mostly, but by no means all, from CCTA).

One book needs a special mention here: *The ITIL Pocket Guide*, published by ITIMF. This is a pocket guide covering the two key components of ITIL – Service Support and Service Delivery. It forms a useful addition to this book, and readers needing a brief background to ITIL should refer to it.

1 Introduction to the IT Infrastructure Library (ITIL)

For many years, the main focus in the IT industry was on applications development. The best people, the biggest budgets and the most systematic thinking were devoted to developing new systems. At this time service management was effectively the 'Cinderella' of IT – a system would be developed and delivered, with little thought given to who would maintain it later.

During the 1980s, however, there were major changes in attitude and practice. In part this was seen in a growing disillusionment with IT among users and an increasing insistence on customer service and value for money. It was realised that many IT systems were never used to their full potential (or even never used at all), and that although most of the budget was actually spent on maintaining existing systems, little formal guidance was available for this activity.

It was within this context that CCTA developed the IT Infrastructure Library. Its purpose was to distil the best practice into a set of guidelines, to become the equivalent to the many methodologies available to systems developers (such as SSADM, SDM etc). It has been a runaway success, and is fast becoming the common language and approach among IT service managers. Over 50,000 books have been sold, and it is used across all industry sectors and in many countries.

ITIL includes both 'above the waterline' services that provide direct services to customers – for example, the Help Desk – and 'below the waterline' services that enable an efficient system to be kept running.

1.1 The ITIL approach

CCTA's primary objective in producing ITIL was to publish a set of comprehensive, consistent and coherent codes of best practice for IT service management, promoting business effectiveness in the use of information systems. A parallel objective has been to encourage the development of supporting services, including:

- appropriate qualifications for professionals working in IT Service Management and the training provision to support those qualifications

- consultancy services to help with the implementation of ITIL conformant practices
- software tools to automate ITIL activities.

ITIL comprises 24 different volumes of guidance on aspects of IT Service Management. These 24 component functions are grouped into sets. The two core sets cover Service Support and Service Delivery.

1.1.1 Service support

Service support is the term given to the related series of functions which provide both stability and flexibility for IT service provision. They are concerned with controlling and facilitating the processes which make the service the right one for the user's business needs. The ITIL approach in this area is one of supporting the customer, not only by offering direct help services, but also by ensuring that appropriate information is held, changes are assessed, approved and tested and that the right software is available. The set comprises five volumes, relating to different elements of the service support process.

Configuration management

Concerned with the identification and control of all the components of the IT service. A key element is the creation of a single repository of data for all the elements of service support. This single data base (known as the Configuration Management Data Base or CMDB) records not only the assets themselves (known as Configuration Items (CIs)) but also the links between them. The CMDB holds information on hardware, software, documentation and networks. While the Configuration Management function is *responsible* for designing and managing the CMDB, it is used by and usually updated by all the service support functions.

Help Desk

The Help Desk is designed as the single point of contact between the IT service providers and users. It will offer advice and guidance in response to queries from users. The Help Desk records all incidents reported, building up an invaluable record for audit and problem analysis.

Problem management

Responsible for taking the incidents identified and recorded by the Help Desk and managing the diagnosis and rectification of the underlying cause. The actual diagnosis is likely to be carried out by others, eg software maintenance, hardware support, but the responsibility for the process rests with Problem Management. The proactive process of preventing problem occurrence and reoccurrence is also their responsibility.

Change management

The management of changes to the IT services and the supporting infrastructure, from the request for change (RFC) through impact assessment, authorisation, building, testing and implementation are all pertinent to this function. IT Services must balance the conflicting issues of facilitating the changes the customers need with the detrimental impacts of inadequately controlled change.

Software control and distribution

Concerned with controlling, storing, distributing and implementing software efficiently and effectively. This role, traditionally a minor one has become central to the health of many organisations IT services, following the move to distributed processing, which requires multiple consistent copies of software throughout an organisation.

1.1.2 Service delivery

Concerned with delivering the right service to customers. Central to this set of functions are the benefits of developing and maintaining formal Service Level Agreements (SLAs). The other functions are the essential underpinning elements which facilitate the SLAs. Again, the ITIL approach is one of identifying the customer need and delivering and supporting that as effectively and efficiently as possible.

Contingency planning

About ensuring the provision of essential IT services in the event of a disaster affecting the computer services. Increasingly this is viewed as a component of Business Continuity Management, concerned with protecting the whole organisation following any disaster.

Cost management for IT services

Covering the establishment and monitoring of the costs incurred in providing IT services. This function is also responsible for any charging of customers for the provision of those services. This is usually under the control of the organisation's financial experts.

Availability management

This function addresses the reliability, serviceability and recoverability of the IT service. Increasingly the need to plan for the correct levels of availability during the acquisition of hardware and software is a prime role of Availability Management.

Capacity management

The most technical of the ITIL functions, it includes capacity planning, sizing and performance management. It is about having the right amount of the right kit at the right time to satisfy business needs.

Service level management

Primarily about the use of service level agreements, which formalise the customers' and providers' expectations of the quality of the IT services to be provided and of the agreed workloads and responsibilities.

1.1.3 The other ITIL sets

Managers' set

Comprising six books covering the whole breadth of IT Service Management. The guidance is aimed at managers responsible for several functional areas. These topics are relevant to all sizes of IT unit, especially the guidance on *Planning and Control* and *Customer Liaison*.

Software support set

Two books concerned with the essential interfaces between those developing and maintaining IT systems and the IT service management functions.

Computer operations set

The guidance in this set is mostly aimed at the large, mainframe type of IT installation.

Networks set

Two books, one dealing with *Network Services Management* and the other – *Management of Local Processors and Terminals* addresses the co-ordination of IT equipment which is physically located in the customers' environment.

1.1.4 Other ITIL services

Qualifications and training

A qualification structure, from an introductory level to an IT Service Manager's certificate has been established by IS examination institutes. The exams are held widely, with several hundred successful candidates. Exams are available in English, from the ISEB; and in Dutch from Exin

Many organisations offer training in support of these examinations. Information on the qualifications, examinations and the availability of training can be obtained from the examination organisations.

ISEB
Information Systems Examination Board
7 Mansfield Mews, London W1M 9FJ
(+44/0) 171 637 2040

Stitching EXIN
Postbus 19147, 3501 DC Utrecht, Netherlands,
(+31/0) 30 344811

Consultancy and automated tools

Various organisations have developed consultancy services in support of the ITIL approach. Similarly a number of automated software tools are available, especially to automate the service support elements of the ITIL philosophy.

1.2 The focus of this text

The full IT Infrastructure Library is written with larger IT units in mind, and indeed some smaller units have not in the past been aware of ITSM skills – although this may change. Figure 1 suggests why this might have been the case, and illustrates the focus of the full ITIL set and of this book.

It shows the different scenarios which arise from combining stability (the number of communications with others) with infrastructure size (hardware, software and number of customers). Some units have low stability, and therefore a particular need for IT service management.

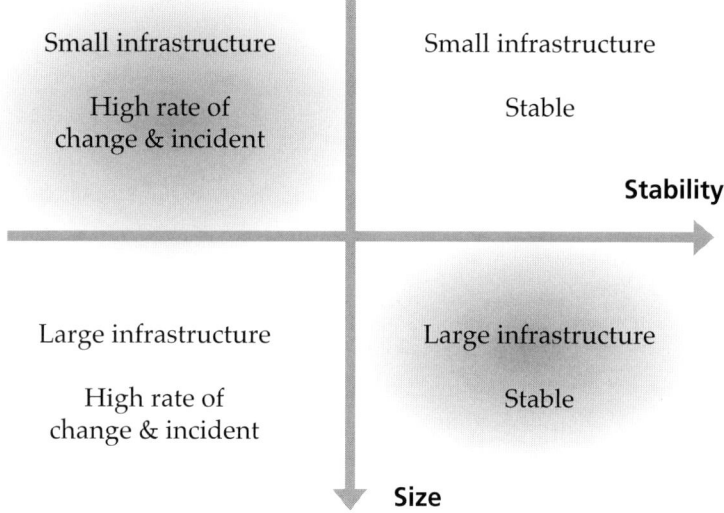

Figure 1: Where you might find SITUs

The top left quadrant

The primary focus for this book is in the top left quadrant: a small, dynamic ITSM unit.

The top right quadrant

In the top right quadrant, stability is the major characteristic. There may be more than one reason why an IT unit finds itself in this position. It could:

- have earned stability by tailoring the IT service to user needs
- be supporting a static customer base
- be part of an organisation which is making very little use of IT.

There may be other reasons, some of which imply an awareness of IT Service management, and others not.

But whatever the reason for the stability, it could change very rapidly due to external influences. Being aware of ITSM will always be of benefit to an IT unit, whatever its size.

The bottom right quadrant

The secondary focus of this book, which is described in Annex E, is for situations where a large infrastructure has matured into a very stable service, and needs only a relatively small staff due to the small number of ITSM communications.

The bottom left quadrant

In the lower left quadrant, mainstream ITIL guidance applies to larger, busier units (who will have specific requirements of their own in applying and adapting ITIL to their environments).

2 The significance of size

There are different perceptions about what constitutes size, and different measurements. Small units can also exist in different circumstances, and have different types of workload and constraints. But small units share more similarities than differences in their culture and in the problems they face. It is important for small IT units to recognise and manage these characteristic features.

2.1 Defining small

Ways of defining 'small' include measuring size and activity to provide a complete picture of the unit's character

It is not easy to find meaningful ways of defining a small IT unit. Not only is every IT unit unique, but also it seems that the variation among smaller units is considerably greater than that among larger units.

2.1.1 Absolute size

Research for this book started by looking at conventional ways to measure size, such as:

- number of staff
- annual budget
- amount of hardware and software
- number of customers.

However, none of these definitions proved to be conclusive. For example, some IT units with 60+ staff considered themselves small, while one unit of 30 staff did *not*. To a large extent, membership of the SITU club was self-determined: an IT unit which *felt* small *was* small.

2.1.2 Relative size

Size can often be a relative measure. For example, some large organisations, especially those who do not rely heavily on IT, have IT units which are relatively small. This can be an uncomfortable situation. When the IT unit represents only a small percentage of the total staff, it can feel small and isolated, with a corporate inferiority complex and trouble in attracting funding.

2.1.3 Stability

One measurement which does seem to be a significant indicator of size is the level of communications between IT Service Management (ITSM) and others. This measurement describes the organisation's *stability*.

In practical terms this can be taken as the number of:

- reported incidents
- requests for change
- contracts with external suppliers and maintainers.

> **Stability**
> The number of interactions carried out. A low number of communications implies high stability, and vice versa

2.2 Characteristics of small and large IT units

It is impossible to make any particular assumptions about the technology which small IT units support – it can be all sorts, including free-standing PCs, a client-server and central minicomputer or a UNIX box with a network around it. Then again, some small units will be supporting stable mainframe-based legacy systems. Indeed it is common for a single unit to combine supporting older mainframe-based services and networked PC-based applications (especially in office automation services).

But whatever the technology, or even the number of staff, small units can be expected to share common characteristics which differentiate them from large ones. These differences can be summed up by comparing the small IT unit to a village, and the larger unit to a city. The relative merits of village and city life have been long debated elsewhere.[1] The important point is that there are fundamental differences which have to be recognised and accounted for. Different *kinds* of approach and solutions are required in each case.

> Small units are like villages – large units are like cities. Each shares the advantages and disadvantages of these different environments

---

[1] Potter (1918)

Figure 2: Village–City comparison

Village	City
Informal culture	Formal culture
Team spirit	Competitiveness
Quick communication	Slow communications
Responsive	Tendency to inertia
Flexible	Constrained
Understanding of the business	Isolation from the business
Relying on individuals	Broad pool of expertise
Nowhere to hide	Role flexibility
Wide knowledge	Specialisms
Limited knowledge	Comprehensive knowledge
High unit costs	Economies of scale
Per capita complexity	Role division

2.2.1 Informal culture

The most noticeable difference between large and small IT units is likely to be one of organisational culture. The village is a close environment where everyone knows or thinks they know everyone else's business. Within a small IT unit there is often a relatively informal atmosphere, as everyone knows everyone else, and what they do or can do.

This contrasts with the city environments of the largest IT units, where procedures and formality are much more important.

However, informality is not always a good thing. It can result in serious risks, especially where disciplines such as configuration management or change management are concerned. Some degree of formality is a necessary part of managing; without it, small IT units can lose control over essential aspects of the service, with very costly results.

2.2.2 Team spirit

Part of the village culture involves making use of cross-specialism contact and support. Reliance on others is the norm, and the unit is likely to see itself as a single team.

This sense of unity contrasts with the city model. Here the environment is large enough to allow a number of internal teams to develop, with possible rivalry between the different IT branches.

2.2.3 Quick communication

Good communication in a small unit is almost inevitable – since each person will be responsible for several roles. Indeed it has sometimes been observed that, in small units, following formal communications procedures would mean people talking to themselves.

In addition, the village-type environment encourages strong informal communications between the IT unit and the business. These links help to ensure that things are done with the minimum number of complications.

In larger organisations, on the other hand, communication is almost always a problem. Everything must be formally recorded and procedures are needed to make sure all the right people are kept in touch with each other.

2.2.4 Responsive

Small IT units can be very responsive, developing and amending plans and procedures as they go. The sheer inertia that goes with large staff numbers is mostly absent, allowing for fast decisions in an environment small enough to canvass everybody's views within a day. This has the benefits of:

- *allowing initiatives to get started with less planning* – this will be interpreted by the customer as a more caring and responsive IT service
- *tailoring ideas during a project or service* – changes are easier because the decision makers are available, and because the staff involved are much more likely to know the requirements and abilities of the rest of the IT unit. Thus changes are more likely to be:
  - made quickly, within a day
  - accepted by other staff
  - tailored to the customers' needs

- *tailoring services to small numbers of staff* – providing a service to 5000 users inevitably means that the users see it as centrally organised and imposed. The small unit working within a small organisation has more chance to personalise its services.

2.2.5 Flexible

Small units can react to changes and new ideas very quickly, benefiting from the village approach to life. Wheeler-dealing is easier as a smaller number of staff means there are plenty of short-cuts available.

If something needs to be discussed or decided, all the major players can probably be brought together in the same room at the same time. New ideas are more likely to at least get attention, and probably support.

And small units can dare to do things which larger units cannot. They encourage a risk-taking approach – not risks to the customer or the service, of course, but risks in the sense of trying out new ideas and approaches.

2.2.6 Understanding of the business

As a final advantage, people who work in small IT units generally have a good understanding of the larger picture, of the organisation's functions, goals and objectives, and of how the IT unit (and ITSM in particular) supports the business functions. They are familiar with user needs and attitudes (especially vital in scientific establishments and their like), and there is greater opportunity for staff to move between the business and IT areas of the organisation. Understanding the business is key to efficiency and effectiveness.

However, small units will require specialists for key functions, who know their customers' business practices and about the latest developments in relevant IT and IS. The inevitable restrictions upon the range of specialists and knowledge the small unit can support, means that they must be carefully tuned to the organisation's needs

Within a large, city type of unit, in contrast, there is more scope for people to concentrate exclusively on one specific area, working in relative isolation from the rest of the unit and of the business. This may have implications for training staff, especially when they face moving from a large IT unit into a smaller one, something occurring more frequently as large organisations fragment under the pressures of outsourcing, downsizing and user empowerment.

2.2.7 Relying on individuals

As well as advantages, however, village life also has its limitations. One of these is the tendency to rely too much on particular individuals – 'heroes' – who may be the only one with the necessary combination of skills and experience to carry out a particular function. For a small IT unit this may be unavoidable, since the decision about how many people to train in a particular role is a balance of cost against risk. Only where there is a major risk to business viability can the cost of training extra people be justified.

It is probably wise to accept that there will be heroes, but to take steps to make the best of the situation:

- try to plan properly for times they will be absent from the office
- ensure they stay up-to-date in their field of expertise, attending relevant training events and conferences
- do what you can to retain them in your organisation, through incentives and job satisfaction.

Small units have to be aware that staff can leave suddenly for a variety of unavoidable reasons, and make sure that functions can survive the departure of any one individual. So while formal communication between separate sections is not usually necessary, it is vital to record what has been decided and what has been done.

2.2.8 Nowhere to hide

A small environment means that if things go wrong, there are fewer options for solving problems. For example when there are personality clashes, there is little that can be done to prevent them from causing damage.

If there are personality clashes in larger units, on the other hand, staff can be moved around to minimise disruption and conflict. Larger units also have the ability to organise people into meaningful groups or sections, allowing them to become more expert in a particular aspect of IT.

2.2.9 Wide knowledge

Another problem that small IT units face is a lack of specialisms.

The village attitude is one of wide knowledge, encouraging those who can turn their hands to anything, or at least favouring those who can pick up new skills or apply familiar concepts to new areas. Most staff have to carry out different roles and are in regular contact with the business. This affects the way a unit is organised, including grading and career paths, and the types of people who feel most comfortable in it.

All IT units have staff who specialise in keeping the infrastructure intact, and service providers who use that infrastructure to provide the agreed levels of service. But a small unit cannot afford many other specialists; the proportions of specialists in particular areas may be the same as for larger units, but absolute numbers are less. Vitally, small units are rarely in a position to have more than one specialist in any given subject area. Thus, both to provide a range of specialist services and to provide cover during staff absences, they are likely to need external suppliers or cross-service arrangements, finding a balance between the need for the specialism, and how long it will be needed for.

Even in very small IT units, there can be particular specialisms that are best dealt with in-house. And as business needs and the technical infrastructure evolves, the skills which are needed will also evolve. IT managers must be ready to acquire new skills as they think appropriate.

The city view, in contrast, is one where a full range of skills can be supported, favouring specialists with a detailed knowledge of a narrower field.

2.2.10 Limited knowledge

Related to its relative lack of specialisms, the village structure also means there are gaps in the knowledge base, since a few people cannot know everything.

To make the most of the skills that are available, small units often have to combine several roles (even potentially separate job functions) within a single post, using staff as generalists rather than specialists. Another way of maximising skills is to let the skills that are actually available define the structure of the unit. This is more efficient than trying to create a structure around a theoretical requirement. As staff change, the structure can be reorganised.

Where skills are not available in-house, small units can make use of specialist services from third-party suppliers, such as outside consultants, rather than trying to cope with their own limited resources. This reduces the specialist skills required within the unit, providing those skills economically for the short time they are needed. This is effectively a decision based on financial considerations. The topic is dealt with in detail in section 3.5.

For the larger IT unit, staff skills and specialisms are available in depth, providing cover for absence and a second opinion on difficult questions.

2.2.11 High unit costs

Village life can be expensive. Small IT units are not in a position to benefit from the economies of scale which may be available to larger units. This means that the total cost to the organisation of employing and supporting each member of IT staff will be higher, reflecting, among other things:

- higher training and skill levels, since staff need to have knowledge of more areas
- higher relative costs of essential software tools.

The cost of IT per user will also be higher, not only for these reasons, but also because:

- hardware and software licence costs will be relatively higher
- relatively more consultancy will be used.

Being large on the other hand brings obvious benefits in economies of scale – obtaining a lower price per unit for goods and services.

2.2.12 Per capita complexity

<small>Small doesn't mean simple: in fact it usually means complex</small>

It is a common misunderstanding that small means simple. In fact many tasks are more complex on a modern small site, not less. Often there will be a greater number of Configuration Item types, no simple terminals (usually PCs, with a wide variety of configurations), and a complex networking infrastructure. If the base infrastructure tools (ie. those supplied with the system software and hardware) are less comprehensive than those in a mainframe environment, then the service management staff will have to expend more effort on activities such as problem resolution, capacity planning, costing and charging. Compared to a larger unit, for each customer (or ITSM staff member) there is likely to be a larger amount of:

- incidents
- configuration items and configuration relationships
- networking software and hardware
- applications, locations and usability issues.

Many small IT units, for example those supporting scientific or research organisations, have a customer requirement that is highly complex and extremely dynamic.

On the other hand some of the simplest IT units are very large, providing a few services to thousands of users. They have their own particular problems but, generally speaking, these are predictable ones. There is no obvious correlation between the difficulty of a job and the size of an IT unit, despite claims from both large and small unit staff that their tasks are inherently more difficult.

2.3 Deciding on the size of an IT unit

There are a number of considerations to take on board when deciding on how to set up an IT unit

Many organisations are faced with options concerning the size of their IT units and also their IT Service Management sections. These options include:

- *a single ITSM function covering all sections of the organisation*
- *multiple, small ITSM operations* – each is tailored to serve a particular part of the business, and located within an operational sub-unit

Outsourcing
Forming contracts with third-party organisations to provide services

- *outsourcing all or part of the IT support service* – if they outsource, organisations need to consider what the optimum size for outsourced units should be. This is likely to be larger rather than smaller, moving towards economies of scale at the cost of specific and relevant service. When small units are outsourced to become part of a larger third-party operation, this will be an almost inevitable result.

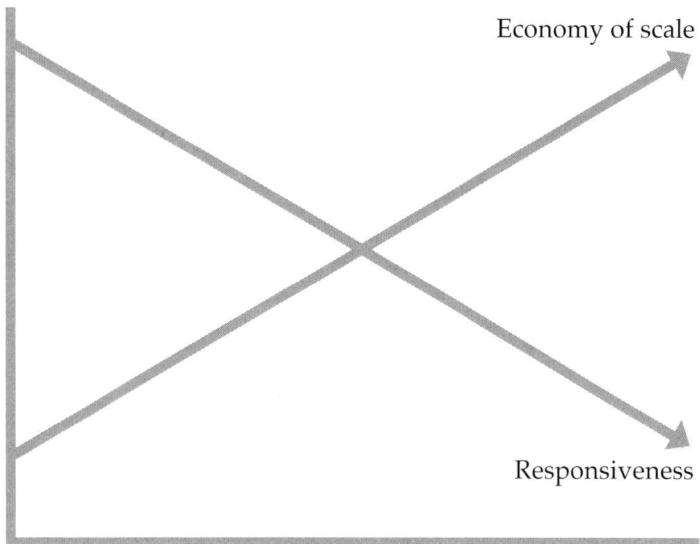

Figure 3: Balance of service and per-capita costs

In practice, the ideal situation for most organisations, whether in-house or outsourced, will lie somewhere between the two extremes of multiple, tiny IT set-ups and a single centralised function. In this way a balance can be struck between the quality of a service tailored to users' needs and economies of scale .

2.4 Scaling down for small IT units

Scaling down ideas to suit small units is sensible practice, but needs to be managed with care

Most managers want to take ideas which have proved valuable elsewhere and try them out in their own environment. This is sensible practice – it is after all the philosophy upon which ITIL is based. However, no two organisations are alike, and, in order to translate ideas successfully from one environment to another, processes and procedures must be adapted to fit.

In this book we are concerned with changes of scale, adapting techniques to smaller units. While some processes scale down easily and function equally well in small or large environments, most will break down if scaled too far.

> 'Process models break down at boundaries of scale'
> *Professor V H Haase, Graz Technical University*

An underlying principle of this book is to consider how scaling down affects the functions in ITIL, and where possible to give ideas for adapting them. The questions to ask about scaling down are:

- is it still practicable?
- is it still desirable?
- do enough of the benefits remain?

If the answer to any of these questions is no, then it is time to find different ways of achieving the same result.

Case example: Supporting Quality Management – a question of scale

Consider an organisation which has introduced the principles of quality management, and has accepted the figure of 3% of staff costs as an appropriate quality management overhead. With around 200 staff, this creates a quality management section of 6 staff, reporting directly to senior management, and independent of the operational management structure (an ISO9000 requirement).

Convert this set-up to smaller establishments.

With 100 staff, the quality section becomes 3 staff, and still functions. With fewer than 50 staff, however, there are problems. In a small unit, 3% of staff costs would translate into one person. This means there is no depth of cover nor contingency for absence; it might also mean two or more people with a part-time role, inevitably compromising the independent reporting requirement.

Alternatives are to:

- spend more than 3% on quality. This leads to a less efficient and competitive organisation and makes the quality function more intrusive
- find alternative ways of providing quality management for 3% of staff costs.

One solution that has worked well, preserving both benefits and budget, is to create regular quality management meetings, rather than a separate quality section. This uses the 3% of staff time by having everyone involved contribute. These meetings send minutes directly to senior management, providing the independent channel required by ISO9000.

Within ITSM, a similar approach might work for scaling down the Change Management function. The Change Manager role could be replaced by a process that requires requests for change (RFCs) to be well costed and passed to all appropriate persons for impact assessment.

Properly managed, scaling down will bring the benefits of ITIL to small IT units.

3 Establishing IT Service Management in small IT units

IT Service Management is just as important in small units as in larger ones. It may even be more complex, as it aims to provide a comprehensive service with limited resources and to extend its influence beyond the IT department into the rest of the business. A necessary part of ITSM in small units will involve creative resourcing using outsiders.

3.1 Setting the ITSM strategy

However small the unit, an ITSM strategy which ties in with the business strategy is very important

The need for a strategic view of IT is not restricted to large units. Even in small ones, it is important to have an IT strategy that is related to the business strategy. The need for such a hierarchical strategy has been well established elsewhere,[2] and relative size will not affect the argument, although moves towards user empowerment, Rapid Application Development and higher rates of business change may well begin to do so.

3.1.1 A simple hierarchical view

In large organisations, the simple hierarchical view of how strategies relate provides a practical model

A simple hierarchical strategy starts with the business strategy of the organisation as a whole. This sets out how business goals and objectives are to be achieved. The IS, IT and ITSM strategies then support these objectives in a direct line relationship.

---

[2] Guidance on developing and maintaining IS strategies is available in CCTA publications

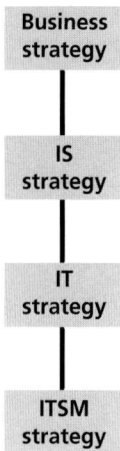

Left Figure 4: a simple view of strategy hierarchy

The business plan should always come first, encapsulating the visions and objectives of the organisation. These are then reflected in the lower level plans, including those for IT Service Management.

In large organisations, formal communication channels between the organisation's various divisions mean that this kind of simple view is more or less valid for everyday use.

3.1.2 A more complex view

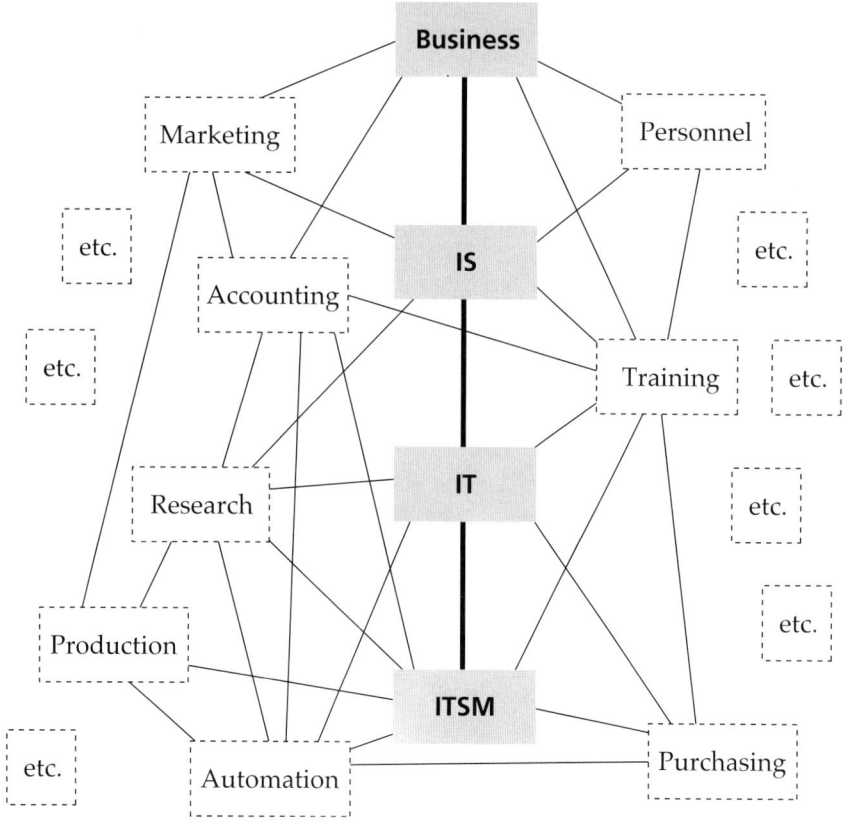

Figure 5: Complex interactions

However, in an age where information systems are pervasive, a simple hierarchical strategy can hide a number of other strategies which will influence IT Services. Particularly in smaller organisations, where IS staff are closer to the business users, the true picture is not so much of direct line departmental relationships, but of multiple overlapping work groups throughout the organisation. Creating an ITSM strategy in this situation may well require a broader awareness and a more flexible view than that implied by the simple hierarchical model.

Of course complexity exists to some degree in all organisations. It depends not only on size, but on many other factors such as:

- the volatility of the market
- the nature of the business
- the attitude of managers.

Nonetheless, managers in small IT units are more likely to need to be aware of all facets of the organisation. Fortunately, in many cases, small size makes it more practical to do this.

The strategies which various parts of the organisation develop will vary in their formality. The trend within IS seems increasingly towards less formally defined strategies for the medium and long term, as users' empowerment and the volatility of business circumstances increases.

3.1.3 Implications of the business strategy for ITSM

Deciding what services to offer depends on what the business is likely to need in the future. The business strategy should give a clue to this – if it does not, or if there is no formal strategy, the IT unit should put its own options to senior management about finding a direction for the service.

Strategic issues which will affect the ITSM strategy include:

- new relationships with customers, leading to the need to collect and analyse information in new ways
- changing demands for management information
- changes in the organisational structure or culture which require new IT capabilities
- moves into new areas of business (forced or voluntary) which need new or changed methods of IT-based support
- changes in business processes (for example from a TQM programme or re-engineering exercise) which require a different level or type of IT support.

3.1.4 Resourcing the ITSM strategy

Since small units rarely have the resources to cover such a wide range of services as larger units, having fewer people means having less cover in specialist areas. The ITSM strategy recognises this by ensuring that essential services are available in-house, with perhaps a few specialisms as well. Other specialist tasks are subcontracted or outsourced, and business units themselves can be encouraged to take on some tasks.

Deciding which specialisms to support in-house is likely to depend on:

- what skills and resources are needed
- how important skills are to the organisation (defined by assessing the risk of not having the skill instantly available when it is needed)
- the cost of buying in skills compared with developing them in-house
- the length of time for which the skills will be required
- the availability and reputation of third-party specialists locally.

Using this kind of logic, it is possible to build up a flexible resource base to support appropriate strategies. In practice, however, greenfield situations are rare, and many ITSM functions will already exist to a greater or lesser extent. So the ideal scenario may well be constrained by current practices.

3.2 Developing the ITSM plan

Drawing up the ITSM plan means setting up a two-way communication cycle with the business plan

The cycle of planning, from a business plan through IS and IT strategies to an ITSM plan, needs to involve a two-way flow of information before the plans can be finalised. The business plan defines business objectives for the planning period: then the ITSM plans feed back any opportunities or constraints from the world of IT, and assigns priorities to competing activities.

3.2.1 Identifying constraints

In a small IT unit feedback to the business plan is especially important because there are likely to be constraints, the effects of which are likely to be more severe than they would be in a larger installation.

Constraints are typically due to:

- available skills
- how well the unit can support any proposed solutions.

Analysing available skills

Skills which affect business and ITSM plans include knowledge of the business and ability to work with users, as well as knowledge of existing IT systems and the technology in use.

Since people in a small unit usually fulfil more than one role, ITSM plans should include training. Although this will be mostly on-the-job, time still needs to be reserved for it. Forward planning estimates should incorporate a target training figure, which can then be monitored using any effort recording system in use.

One important area for training is in the techniques of skills and knowledge transfer. This will reduce reliance on individuals and is an essential form of insurance against loss of key skills.

Developing Support

A point to remember, when ITSM planning is underway, is that the demand for support as well as for software and hardware will be much greater when IT systems are distributed round more than one site, even if the architecture supporting them is simple.

Much of this extra support can be met by using layered support and appointing users as Local Systems Administrators (LSAs). The LSAs will also take on much of the day-to-day running of local systems.[3] However, the time spent by users acting as LSAs is a real IT cost to the organisation, even though it may not appear in the IT unit's budget, and this should be recognised.

Local Systems Administrators (LSAs)
User representatives responsible for the day-to-day running of their IT and acting as a focus for incidents. They provide local first-line support to users

3.2.2 Assigning priorities

Because of these constraints, the ITSM plan needs to assign priorities. In a small IT unit, as in any other, the key priority must always be to meet business aims and objectives.

It is important to remember that current services and equipment are actually delivering business benefits now; so, supporting the current infrastructure must take priority over plans for replacement. And common sense suggests that an organisation which cannot support its current practices is unlikely to be successful with enhancements to them. All plans must reflect the accepted priorities

---

[3] The LSA role is described in the *Managing Local Processors and Terminals* volume of ITIL.

of the work done by the unit, or for which the unit is responsible. These might be:

1. supporting existing IT systems and software packages
2. supporting users, for example with help desk and problem solving facilities
3. buying in any packages which are needed
4. managing subcontracted work
5. managing bespoke development work.

A common error among IT units in setting priorities is to be too concerned with protecting against errors, at the expense of providing benefits:

> *'Removing all the possible causes of failure does not automatically deliver success'* Paul Herzlich, Système Evolutif

Users will often tolerate problems with a service if it still helps them with their work and brings positive business benefits.

A relevant analogy would be with car ownership; no matter how well matched a car is to someone's needs, the owner will be able to find something about it they dislike. This will not prevent them from using the car, nor from a repeat purchase of the same model. What is important to the driver is what the car *does* do, rather than what it doesn't. The same is true in IT Service Management.

For allocating restricted resources to multiple tasks, there is a simple technique which can be used to assess priorities and balance resources against what people need and want.

---

1. Identify all the tasks for which the unit is responsible.
2. Establish what resources are required for each, typically expressed in man-weeks per financial year.
3. List tasks in priority order, with the resources they will need.
4. Count down the resources column, until the total reaches the resources available.
5. Draw a line here. This represents the work that can be done.

    If there are tasks below the line which are vital, a new solution must be found.

3 Establishing IT Service Management in small IT units

In order to be valid, this assessment does not have to be carried out in great detail – most of the benefit (that is, a picture of what *is* actually possible) will come from a quick, broad-brush approach. However, the process is inevitably more complicated than it seems at first sight because:

- *the process is iterative* – the impact of not doing tasks which initially lie below the line often requires a rethink of priorities
- *priorities are influenced by customers* – customers may be willing to fund some tasks and not others, either directly, if there is a charging system, or indirectly through approval at financial committees. Customer opinions in these circumstances are not always easy to predict
- *resources may not be evenly spread* – an ITSM unit may find itself with apparently spare resources but with too much work for the only people capable of doing it.

3.3 Agreeing and delivering the IT service

> At the heart of ITSM is the responsibility for agreeing and delivering what customers want

For any IT Service Management function, the answer to the key question 'What am I in business *for?*' is 'to provide a service to the organisation'. This primary responsibility does not depend on the size of the IT unit. However, some aspects of agreeing and delivering the service are unique to small IT units.

3.3.1 Relationships with customers

The service must keep its customers happy and respond to their needs. This means knowing who they are, whether internal or a mixture of internal and external, what they want and what they need. This also means knowing how to prioritise their demands. ITSM should be more than a passive instrument, and use ways of adding value to customer service without over-stretching its resources. For example:

- the Help Desk knows where local services can be found outside the unit and can give advice to customers about available options
- ITSM can communicate to customers:
    - about the different things they want, itemising those they can have
    - what the priorities for service provision are (internally or by other means such as cross-service agreements)
    - its performance against agreed service levels

- customers can make suggestions for improving the service, which are noted and taken up where possible.

3.3.2 Documenting and supporting the service

ITSM relies on formal, documented relationships with customers and suppliers

The size of an ITSM unit is not likely to make any major difference to the need to be clear about the precise services on offer. The basic principles apply:

- knowing which services ITSM is responsible for supplying and supporting
- defining, so far as is reasonable, the levels of service required
- ensuring that both supplier and customer share the same view of the service.

Service level agreements

Service level requirements, expressed in terms which are comprehensible to customers, are documented and monitored in Service Level Agreements (SLAs).

The waterline
The lowest level of detail of relevance to the customer is called the waterline. Above are the services customers use, expressed in their terms. Below are technicalities, for IT people to deal with

The IT unit is always responsible for meeting performance goals in SLAs, subject only to customers fulfilling their obligations. Parts of the service may be provided by consultants, subcontractors or other parts of the organisation (for example network support, application maintenance or office services). The Service Level Management function must also make sure that the requirements within the SLAs are supported by underpinning contracts. The illustration shows the concept of a 'waterline'; activities below the line are for ITSM to deal with. The customer in turn relies on ITSM to deliver the service efficiently, economically and reliably.

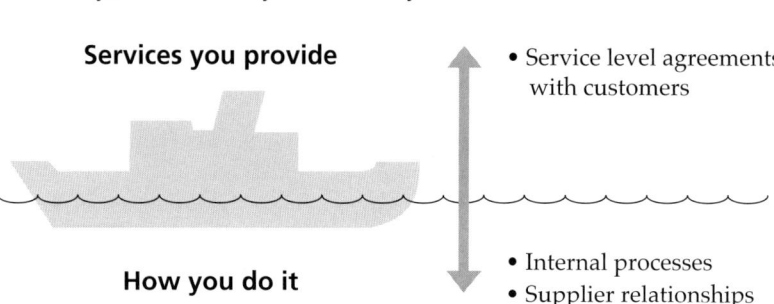

Figure 6: the waterline

3.3.3 Relationships with suppliers

Relationships with suppliers often play an important part in providing an effective service. The formal aspect of the relationship with suppliers (both internal and external) is not enough, however, essential though it is. Small units generally depend on suppliers' goodwill and must cultivate it, although without being subservient – they should aim for an equal partnership.

Building a good relationship means:

- providing suppliers or sub-contractors with the right information for the job, even beyond the demands of the contract
- listening to suggestions constructively and acting on them, unless they cause problems with the service
- sharing knowledge of the service fully so that suppliers know what to aim for
- recommending suppliers to others if they do a good job. In return, expecting them to provide excellent service and product leadership, even beyond the formal demands of the contract.

The contract acts as an assurance that there is, as a last resort, a way of resolving disputes, for use only when all other avenues are closed. It is useful to document the non-contractual relationship as well; this ensures a common understanding of requirements, procedures and so on. (This might be called a working practices document).

Documentation

If suppliers are to work with forms, guides, practices and conventions, they should be involved in producing and maintaining them. They are likely to have wide experience of documentation, based upon several sites, and will have useful views to consider.

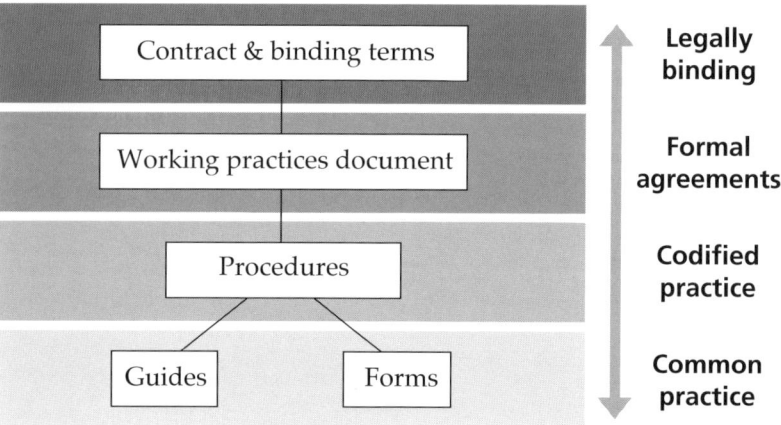

Figure 7: Documentation hierarchy

One organisation, having established a new single-source hardware maintenance contract, spent considerable time devising a control procedure. This procedure used newly designed, multiple copy forms, and laid down authorities for approval and constraints upon the engineer's authority.

When the contract was in place, it transpired that the supplier's own in-house procedures and paperwork, built upon years of experience, were easier to understand, more comprehensive and cheaper to operate. Pride dictated that the new, cumbersome procedure was used, until the suppliers asked for extra money to compensate for the extra time and effort their staff needed to use it!

It is worthwhile documenting less tangible aspects of the contract too, such as ideas and ideals. Even though suppliers can only promise to try to fulfil them, writing them down provides both sides with an agreed basis of intention, stability and common language.

The need for documentation applies equally to any mutually beneficial agreements made with any other organisations. A real danger here is to be too informal, relying on good will between individuals who may leave at short notice. Put any such agreements on a firm basis with a contract expressing the requirements of the SLA(s), just as for a supplier or sub-contractor. Successful relationships of this kind are not common; they rely on two or more organisations having a sufficiently similar approach to an aspect of ITSM to be able to work together for a common benefit. Circumstances which might encourage their use include:

- organisations with similar but non-competing objectives, such as government departments
- situations where joining together creates buying power for things such as consumables, hardware or consultancy.

3.3.4 Organising the unit to meet service goals

The way responsibilities are assigned in the unit should support its service provision in three ways:

- one person should ultimately be accountable for each service, no matter who contributes to providing it
- the process by which services are delivered should have the minimum of hand-overs across the organisation and no unnecessary steps. Hand-overs can be eliminated by reorganising functions and processes at the same time (organising ITIL functions in small units is dealt with later in this guide)
- similar work should be passed to the same skills groups, making the most of people's abilities and experience (the same knowledge, skill, experience; similar data and results; triggered by the same event with the same timing).

Sometimes these responsibilities, particularly the second and third, are contradictory. Nonetheless, the organisation should work in such a way as to reconcile them as well as possible. An important part of organising efficiently is ruthlessly eliminating unnecessary work – if a task does not contribute directly to the service, it should be eliminated.

Prime candidates for elimination are tasks which:

- are generated by unnecessary steps in the process
- are designed for completing forms which are filed, never to be used again
- don't contribute to fulfilling SLAs.

Within a small ITSM unit, there will not be spare capacity to carry any unnecessary tasks and their profile will be higher, making them more easily identifiable.

3.4 Extending Service Management beyond IT

ITSM disciplines can extend beyond IT into support for essential business functions as well

IT Services Management is well positioned to offer more than an IT support service alone. ITIL functions employ skills which can support essential business functions as well, such as office services, project management, training and personnel. ITSM can act as a channel for delivering a whole range of business support to the user, including helping customers who are developing their own applications on end-user equipment.

By combining the services management of a number of business functions, both the customer and the organisation as a whole stand to benefit from:

- economies of scale
- consistency across a wide range of customer concerns
- a better use of customer-facing staff and their particular skills.

While analogies with predators and prey are not always helpful, it can help morale if small IT units see themselves as predatory in the sense of extending their area of work, rather than being worried about encroachment from outside. This also helps people to understand the very real possibility of work being outsourced.

Targeting a wider area than IT services means that much more of the business benefits from the service management disciplines. In turn, this strengthens the case for expenditure on software tools, staff training and change. For many organisations, broadening the base of those who benefit is a vital element of the ITSM cost/benefit equation.

In small organisations, the IT unit is often well placed also to extend its services to areas where its expertise, experience and resources are relevant. This requires no grand plan: it can happen as opportunities present themselves. Perhaps a service offered to one part of the business can be used (in a different way) by others – new, creative uses for a service are always useful. Or perhaps the skills of the IT unit can be used to help other parts of the business improve their own performance. If time is available, people can be released to help train others; perhaps staff from other business units can be seconded to ITSM to learn and at the same time help the IT unit. This can be demonstrated by considering:

- Help Desk
- Service Level Management.

3.4.1 Extending the Help Desk function

An IT Help Desk provides a single point of contact for users to report IT incidents of any kind. This means that users have a familiar and easily reached contact point whether the problem is software, hardware, telecoms, documentation or training. Users do not have to be able to decide what the problem is before they can get appropriate help.

But the Help Desk does not have to be limited to IT problems. With the integration of IT into the office environment, users are often unsure if their problems are caused by IT or something else. They can be confused about who to contact, resulting in delays in sorting out their problem.

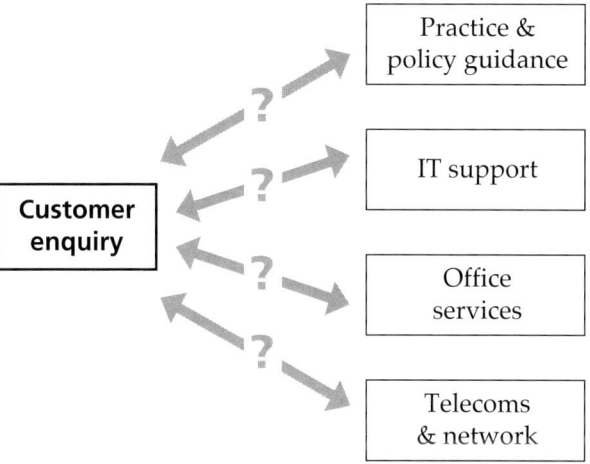

Figure 8: Situation with support services independent

This situation can be improved by expanding the scope of the Help Desk to receive and log all incidents that affect the user, whatever their cause. The user then knows where to call for help in case of difficulty. Clearly users benefit, but ITSM also benefits because:

- the wider service means economies of scale, and may mean full-time staff for the Help Desk. This results in:
  - easier coverage of the shift
  - back-up for staff absence
  - more justification for investing in support tools

- reduce the need for (as much) bought-in resource in future similar circumstances

- clarify and simplify future discussions with external specialists (due, in part at least, to an understanding of the terms and principles involved)

- improve staff morale by broadening of individuals' skills and understanding.

Problems with skills transfers can be that they:

- take up so much time and effort that they get in the way of the job and/or result in unforeseen extra expenditure

- are pursued because staff members are interested solely for their own sakes (that is, they are succumbing to technical curiosity).

3.5.2 Cross-servicing

Cross servicing
Two similar IT units provide services for each other

Two IT units in the same town or district, with a similar IT infrastructure and some common needs may decide that they can do a better job for their users by providing each other with particular services. Examples of cross-servicing might include off-site storage, or providing facilities for hardware maintenance such as engineers' stores and accommodation.

3.5.3 Recommendations for working with external suppliers

Organisations should consider using external suppliers if:

- they have to invest a great deal of effort or skills to maintain specialist services; in this case they should stick to basic, common services

- the alternative is employing people who can only do one specialised job which is rarely needed.

If work does go out to external suppliers, contracts must reflect the service agreements the IT unit has signed with the business. Contracts must include all aspects of standards and legislation which are needed to deliver the services concerned.

3.6 Developing the service

> ITSM ideas aren't restricted to IT. they can provide a wider business service if resources allow

IT Service Management can do much more than run computers. As we have seen, it should also support the organisation's business objectives. To do this, it can:

- provide a *business* service
- add more value to the *business as a whole*
- establish connections through the business so that if the IT unit doesn't know the answer, it knows who does – and in a full sense *provide information.*

But the wide choice of services the IT unit could supply is constrained by limited resources. How should the choice be made?

The core service is providing IS and, from these systems, support to the business. Without this, the unit will not have a firm foundation of satisfactory performance. SLAs should start from here.

It may be that resources are so tight that nothing else is possible, though this seems unlikely. In any case plans should always assume that existing resources of all kinds can be better used. Without such pressure there is little tangible incentive to improve performance, resulting in missed opportunities. And units which keep missing opportunities are less likely to survive.

Usually there are ways to get better results:

- parts of internal processes – steps, forms, files and so on – can be eliminated, so reducing the workload
- some services can be prioritised by referring to existing Business, IT and IS plans (see section 2.2). This is a two-way process, since IT and IS plans should be made with reference to constraints of staff and skills.

Those positive ways of focusing the service should help to balance resource constraints.

The ultimate judge of ITSM is customer perception. So ITSM must be continually aware of it, and also of the pressures customers face – their attitudes and concerns. The service should take every opportunity to add value over and above the core services it provides and remain, as much as possible, aware of business trends.

Those most likely to be in touch with customers are often the more junior people, who for instance man the help desk, audit assets and so on. Their proximity to customers can be a very useful source of contacts and ideas.

3.7 ITSM and the IT infrastructure

ITSM can influence planning for the IT infrastructure by putting concerns about architecture, cost and reliability on the agenda

Decisions about planning an IT Infrastructure are strategic, and affect the whole organisation, not just ITSM. Thus the most ITSM can hope to do is to influence these strategic decisions.

Aspects of IT infrastructure planning which have a major influence on ITSM include:

- *minimum spread* – this means making a *strategic architectural choice* very early, selecting a hardware configuration (say Apple, IBM, UNIX, DEC, H-P) and a choice of software (Windows, Windows-NT, DOS, OS/2, X-OPEN) at the same time.
- *reliability* – service delivery depends on locally available support. If the unit cannot tackle much that is complex, a good call-out response time is important.
- *cost* – even today, the IT architecture may well need to perform over a long time period. So whole lifecycle costs need to be considered. Features which influence cost include:
   - charges for maintenance
   - ease of maintenance
   - expected failure rates
   - durability and maintainability of software
   - depreciation costs and possible resale values
   - upgrade ability – will it be obsolete after 24 months or can it be upgraded?

4 Managing a small IT unit

The principles involved in managing an IT unit are more or less the same, regardless of size. However, making sure that small units are organised to carry out all the services required of them, and making sure they have the skills to do so, can present some particular management problems.

4.1 Adopting a hands-on approach

Managers of small units generally need a hands-on approach

The major difference in a small unit is that managers have to have a much more hands-on approach to data gathering, especially the compilation of appropriate information.

Some managers might see this as a problem, but there are advantages:

- proximity to the work means managers have a better understanding of the real needs and wants of customers and IT staff
- managers stay closely in touch with staff and the day-to-day issues affecting the unit and the organisation
- there is less likelihood of data gathering for the sake of it
- management is more flexible and changes of practice easier.

4.1.1 Keeping time records

One particular aspect of a hands-on approach to management is knowing how people spend their time. This takes effort, but it is justifiable in specific circumstances. It is, however, more useful to concentrate on recording output – results – rather than input – time, and to encourage staff to improve estimating by recording time personally. Time is then planned on the basis of a 'full shop', with everyone fully occupied and their commitments entered in the diary of activity for the unit.

4.3.1 Single-source maintenance agreements

Single source maintenance
Where an IT unit passes on all the responsibility for dealing with suppliers to a third party

It may be possible to pass the whole problem on to a third party who will take responsibility for all the infrastructure components and all the suppliers. This gains leverage, since the third party will have other sites and thus more influence and a higher priority with suppliers. Small units should make sure that these advantages are passed on to them if they do make such an agreement.

There are disadvantages, however. The unit may lose hands-on control. Upgrading may be more complex because the maintenance agreement has to be taken into account. And the unit has to rely on an outsider for critical aspects of the service. Such agreements must be managed through carefully constructed contracts which draw down from the agreed SLAs.[4]

4.3.2 Joint maintenance agreements

Joint maintenance
Where small units combine together to make a joint maintenance agreement

An alternative is for two or more IT units to make a joint maintenance agreement with suppliers. This means keeping control while gaining some leverage. But agreements can be hard to reach, and need good contacts and, above all, close co-operation to work well.

4.4 Managing administration

Administration is an important part of ITSM which needs to be fully resourced, perhaps from outside the unit

Administration is an essential part of any efficient organisation which supports and enables progress rather than obstructing it. There are essential ITSM administrative tasks integral to an IT unit, even a small one.

Experience shows that small units need to allocate at least 10% of staff numbers to administration. With less, others have to take the load or leave essential administration undone. Either way the service suffers.

All ITSM tasks include an element of administration. It is not restricted to basic tasks such as filing, but covers more general support work, including keeping minutes of meetings, forms and process management, quality system administration and producing management information.

---

[4] Refer to the ITIL Module *Third Party and Single-source Maintenance* for a full discussion of this topic.

In many organisations most day-to-day users will be in administrative grades. This opens up considerable opportunities for both the IT unit and the business, for example:

- appointing administration staff in IT who have current knowledge of the business
- exchanging staff between business and IT units, establishing friendly contact between the two environments
- building up a reservoir of IT literate staff.

An enlightened unit may well make use of such staff for more than administrative purposes, for example for establishing the potential or real usability of new or changed services (and not just the IT components).

5 Creating an organisational structure for ITSM in small IT units

The IT Services Manager within a small IT unit has to make sure that all tasks are covered with only a small number of staff. In most cases the number of identified roles within ITSM will be more than the number of people in the unit.

5.1 Allocating tasks for ITSM

IT services managers will need to identify the best way of carrying out the tasks which support the IT needs of the business. Only a minority of essential ITSM functions are intrinsically better done in-house. The options for delivering the various tasks within ITSM can be set out as follows.[5]

ITSM provides	Services that need to be retained in-house and performed by the IT Services section
ITSM jointly provides	Services that can be delivered by IT Services in partnership with another provider (this may be third-party, application development or business units)
Business provides	Services that are best supplied by staff within the business function (although the cost may still be seen as part of supporting IT within the organisation)
Third party provides	Services that are best outsourced to external service providers
Developer provides	Services that can be supplied by the application development staff or system procurement staff.

Of course each IT unit is unique, so although the advice given here applies generally to small IT units, there will be exceptions.

---

[5] Detailed proposals for meeting ITSM requirements, arrived at by analysing individual components of ITIL functions, and the most likely source for each, are presented in Annex B.

Each IT Services Manager must consider:
- what IT services are dictated by the needs of the business
- constraints applying within the organisation
- skills that will be needed to provide services
- skills available
- the budget.

Figure 10 illustrates a logical approach to deciding which tasks should be done within IT Services, and which should be done elsewhere.

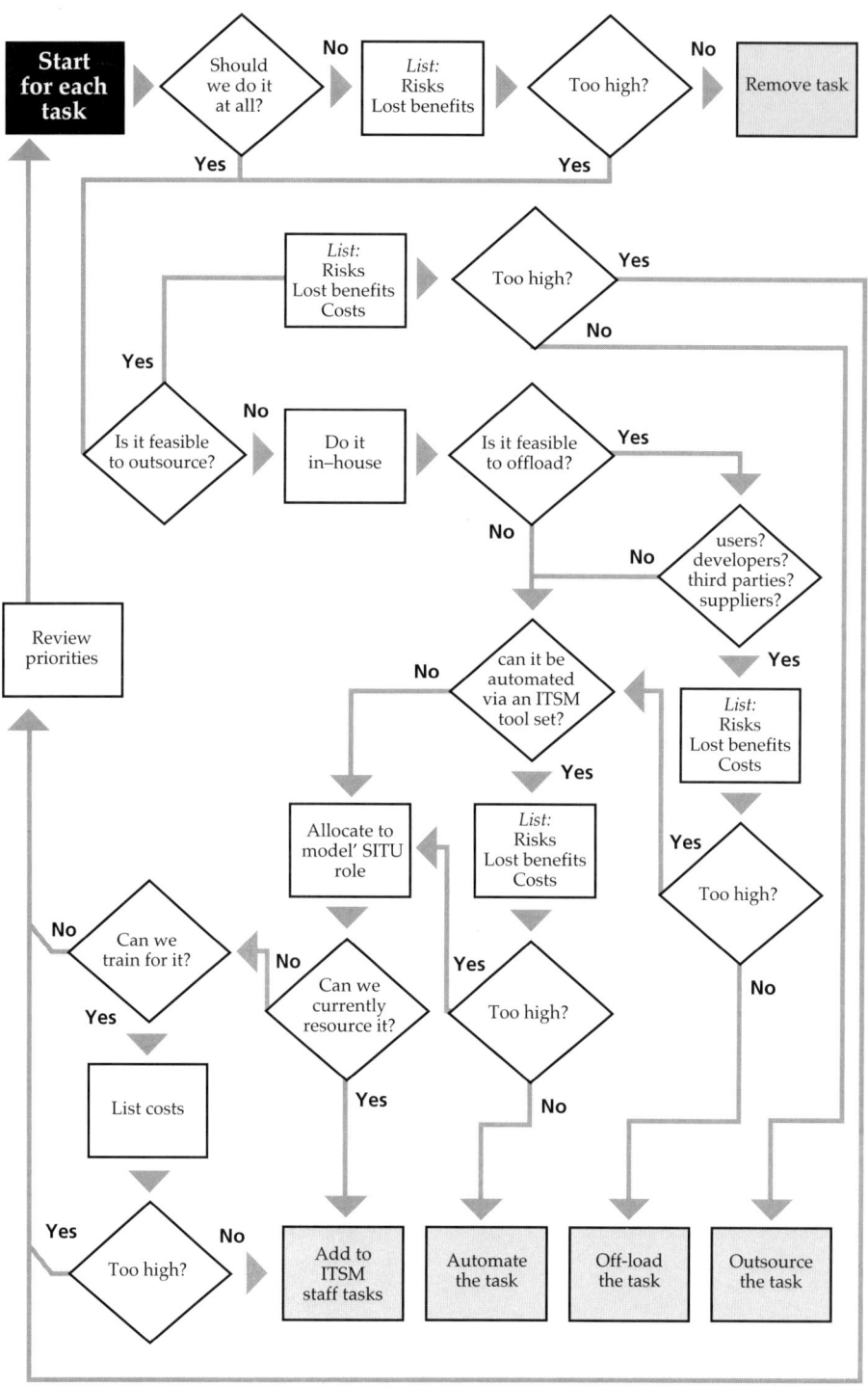

Figure 10: Algorithm for deciding what tasks should be done by whom and with what support.

5.1.1 Underlying Assumptions

The steps within the algorithm are based upon some underlying assumptions about the organisation and how it interfaces with others.

Assumption 1

The developers or procurers of in-house systems know (and care about) what happens in all stages of the system lifecycle, including the service delivery stage.

If they do not, they will neither be able nor willing to take responsibility for problem solving and prevention.

Assumption 2

There are close links in place with suppliers or maintainers of all the infrastructure elements (particularly network and software components), preferably electronic.

Assumption 3

Management reporting and metrics-gathering are automated. Support tools help to deal with ad-hoc, complex queries and with the production of time-based reports (for example weekly reports on the status of change requests). Suppliers are committed to implementing initial queries and to providing ongoing support for changes.

Assumption 4

Help Desk can provide cover for user calls.

This can be achieved in either of two ways:

- increasing the breadth of services offered outside IT
- off-loading simpler tasks to Local Systems Administrators (LSAs) and increasing the level of skill of people on the Desk so that they can handle a greater percentage of complex incidents. This will also help to build close liaison with second line support.

Assumption 5

The extra risks to services (and possibly lost benefits) which ensue from allowing developers, third-party staff and business users a greater role (for example access to ITSM databases) are acceptable.

5.2 Scaling down ITSM roles for full-time staffing

Small units have to find ways of combining the ITIL roles to suit their resources

Each ITSM function can be seen as an assembly of component tasks. ITIL explains how these combine into mainstream ITSM roles. However, this structure needs to be reconsidered for small IT units. Assuming that as many tasks as possible are dealt with outside ITSM (including application developers, the business and third parties), the structure below suggests how scaling down can be achieved.

ITSM Role within a SITU	Approach to the role	Where the role should reside
Role 1 Problem and Availability Management	Establish close links with sources of support outside the unit, but keep responsibility	Some tasks done outside ITSM, but mainly within business unit
Role 2 Help Desk	Outsource (perhaps partly) to the business through LSAs *or* expand scope to provide a business Help Desk	Some tasks done outside ITSM, but mainly within business unit
Role 3 Configuration Management Change Control Software Control & Distribution	Reduce assessment role of Change Manager (Change Advisory Board more active). Change Manager role may be redundant – increase scope of the Change Initiator role.	Some tasks done outside ITSM, but mainly within business unit
Role 4* Costing and Capacity	Outsource on ad-hoc basis for performance exercises, modelling, establishing plans	Mostly done by consultancy (some mechanics remain internal)
Role 5* Contingency	Outsource or join with security or Business Continuity Management (depends upon organisation's risks and maturity)	Mostly done by consultancy (some mechanics remain internal)
Role 6 Service Level Management Help Desk Management Charging	Provide core ITSM for customer-facing service	Keep in-house

* not recommended as in-house ITSM roles.

Key points to note here are:

- most tasks shown as candidates for outsourcing could equally well be carried out in-house even in a small unit. The exception is likely to be the specialist occasional tasks such as capacity planning
- all ITIL functions involve set-up tasks, implementing new procedures, post-implementation review and ongoing monitoring and audit. Establishing these will probably depend on consultancy support, whether or not the function is going to be performed in-house
- deciding which tasks to keep in-house and which to outsource will depend upon the skills which are available both inside and outside the small IT unit.

5.3 Adapting roles in-house

> Each combined role depends on flexible staff attitudes and a realistic assessment of what is actually possible

This section looks in detail at how to combine and adapt the six roles within the confines of a small unit.

The major influences on how those roles are actually performed include:

- staff attitudes, making possible overlap, cross-function working and mutual support (or interference) between ITIL functions
- restrictions on scope, both because of limitations imposed by staffing and finance, and because the complexity and rigour appropriate for mainstream ITIL functions will not be so necessary.

Additionally there are aspects of ITSM which apply to all sizes of unit, but which are particularly visible within a small one where they are also often easier to deal with. Examples include user education and awareness, where a more flexible approach can be taken when dealing with smaller numbers.

In many ways, small IT units are in a position to benefit most from increased technology to automate processes, relieving the load on staff. Automation can be a way of offering a full-time process, even when the function itself is only staffed part-time.

5.3.1 Role 1: Problem and Availability Management

At first sight these two functions may seem unrelated – in mainstream ITIL terms, Problem Management is in Service Support and Availability Management is part of Service Delivery. However, they share a commitment to a proactive, forward looking and inventive approach. In fact good availability management can be said to be reflected by the absence of availability problems – within acceptable cost limits, of course.

Within a small unit, this is a good example of how to build a job around tasks which require similar skills. Application development staff will have much of the expertise needed to prevent problems, especially software ones, and to manage availability. There should already be close liaison with them for:

- building in good availability
- fixing faults as they occur.

It is a small but sensible step to extend this liaison to draw up proactive availability and problem management measures. This is facilitated by the village atmosphere of the small IT unit, where ITSM and applications development will see, hopefully, that they share a common purpose.

ITSM should, however, be aware that final responsibility for these measures must remain with them. If not, there is a very real danger that supporting live services will take second place to the development of new ones.

5.3.2 Role 2: Help Desk

In small IT units, Help Desk staff are more aware of how the unit operates, and can interpret this for their customers.

Where there is a wide diversity of users, either geographically or of specialisms, it makes sense to identify Local Systems Administrators (LSAs) from user staff. Selecting LSAs:

- lightens the load for the ITSM Help Desk
- provides users with someone familiar with their working environment as a first point of contact
- filters out trivial and multiple incidents.

In order to keep an accurate picture of customer concerns and incidents, LSAs should log all the incidents they receive and resolve. This will be more feasible if they have access to the software support tool on which incidents are logged.

Help Desk codes of conduct

Help Desks see themselves as the single point of contact between customers and IT Services: however, business managers and customers see them as the contact point for the whole of the IT unit. In order to fulfil that role, Help Desks must adopt a code of conduct which specifies:

- never blaming other parts of the IT unit for any problems
- accepting comments, suggestions and complaints about any aspect of the IT directorate's service, logging them, and channelling them to the right person
- having enough knowledge to understand such calls, or making sure that the customer is contacted by someone else who does.

Coping with a part-time Help Desk role

In a small IT unit, it will probably not be possible to justify manning the Help Desk full-time. What often happens is that the people responsible for taking Help Desk calls work on other things as well. However, they are then constantly interrupted – the very thing the Help Desk system was designed to avoid. Section 3.4.1 looked at the potential for widening the Help Desk's coverage to provide a business service. Other techniques that may help include:

- *using the GP technique* – full Help Desk services are available at set times – that is, 'surgery hours'; an answerphone and emergency contact number are available for the rest of the working day. This at least reduces the level of interruption to IT staff, but it does rely on understanding customers
- *using the spare time of Help Desk staff for proactive work* – this might involve:
  - making telephone or electronic remote audits of IT or any other assets
  - notifying users of any new changes or workarounds
  - contacting users to check satisfaction or just to keep in touch
  - updating manuals and documentation – the Help Desk is in a good position to judge users' levels of understanding and comprehension
- *introducing automation* – this can be done by using intelligent telephone systems, that would give callers options for example:

  - press 2 for news about the current situation (perhaps the network is down and will be restored in 30 minutes; which will explain many users' problems)
  - press 9 to record a message logging your incident which will be dealt with in due course
  - press 0 to talk to someone in an emergency.

Getting the Help Desk process right

Procedures should be no more complicated than they need to be and reflect *customers'* perceptions of incidents and problems, rather than ITSM's. For example, a complex structure of incident classification is not necessary. Although ITIL recommends 7 levels, in practice 3 levels of priority is all people will feel comfortable with. Using three levels for categorising wounded men in wartime (triage), for example, has been well established for thousands of years.

How incidents are ranked must reflect their impact upon the business they support, and not to ITSM criteria. For example, a broken printer is just a routine incident to IT. However, to the business it could be very serious, if important month-end printing was taking place. To make ranking criteria clear, everyday language should be used to describe the priority levels, for example:

Priority Level 1	I can't do something important
Priority Level 2	Please fix as soon as you can, but I can get on with something else for now
Priority Level 3	I can live without it for a while.

5.3.3 Role 3: Configuration management, Change management and Software control and distribution

The combination of Configuration Management, Change Control and Software Control & Distribution is sometimes known as the *greater change* role. That is, it deals with defining the infrastructure configuration, and controlling or carrying out changes to it. Where multi-tasking is necessary, this group of roles represents a logical combination.

This is, in many ways, the counterpoint to Role 1 – Problem Management and Availability Management. It deals with reactive responsibilities, and is very much a back-room job which forms the foundation of IT service management, for without accurate basic data, ITSM cannot perform effectively.

In many small units, taking the full ITIL approach to configuration management will not be worthwhile – the overheads of establishing and maintaining the configuration links will be too great. However, it is still essential to record assets accurately in some way.

When change requests are received, a small unit may well be able to assess them without using a designated change manager, by setting up and documenting appropriate consultation processes instead. Meetings to assess and decide on any debatable change requests and to assign priorities will still be needed, usually chaired by the IT Services Manager.

If the organisation as a whole has formal change control procedures with which the IT unit complies, any major changes can be dealt with under them. This has the advantages of:

- making sure that the organisation as a whole is involved in any changes to working practices
- considering the impact of change requests for the business as a whole, not just the ITSM or even IS aspects
- using a single, universally understood approach and a uniform set of documents.

5.3.4 Role 4: Costing and capacity management

These tasks are so specialist that most small units would not normally find it economical to keep them in-house. Units have a choice of either spending over the odds or using third-party support: in both cases, in-house work will be needed to carry out the roles on a day-to-day basis. Establishing costing and capacity management is normally done through consultancy.

Cost management

All organisations need to know what each of its IT services costs. This information allows them to:

- make sound judgements on the financial justification for requests for change and enhancements
- determine whether the service offers value for money, when cost is compared against usage
- identify high-cost services to target for cost reduction.

However, establishing accurate costing is expensive and resource intensive. To keep costs to a minimum, small IT units need to establish carefully the degree of accuracy they really need. They must resist the temptation to introduce more complex and expensive schemes. If the point of the scheme is to identify the cost of providing services to customers, most of the information can be derived from a relatively inaccurate system.

The Pareto principle
This is one of the many occasions when 80% of the decisions and results will flow from 20% of the theoretically available data

The golden rule is keep it simple. Start with basic measures and introduce more detail as and when it is needed.

Once the costing system is up and running, maintaining it will require:

- software monitoring tools
- a staff time recording system
- an analysis of the measures which have been observed.

Capacity management

Many small units spend a large part of their ITSM resources on supporting office automation software running across networked PCs. There are very few capacity management tools and techniques for this – getting by depends on common sense and feedback from users.

On larger platforms (anything from UNIX up to mainframes) all aspects of capacity management such as capacity planning, monitoring hardware usage or tuning systems, need experts who are highly skilled in dealing with the particular platform, as well as expensive monitoring software. Even medium-to-large organisations will probably not invest in this expertise and equipment, which is only needed for a few weeks each year.

5.3.5 Role 5: Contingency Planning

In small organisations, the IT unit is probably integrated physically with the rest of the organisation. So it is counter-productive to consider how to recover the IT service in isolation. Any disaster will affect the business as a whole and planning for it should consider business continuity on an organisational level. ITSM must obviously consider its own needs following a disaster, but it should do this as a member of the BCM (Business Continuity Management) team.[6]

5.3.6 Role 6: Service Level management, Help Desk management, Charging

With all services, the key to establishing, measuring and delivering the correct level of service is the documented agreement on what is to be provided. This is important but often difficult to establish in a small environment, where there is likely to be a tradition of informality and providing services in an ad-hoc fashion.

---

[6] BCM is described in section 7.2

Hierarchical Service Level Agreements (SLAs)

To simplify the amount of negotiation needed to set up SLAs in a small but complex organisation, such as, for example, a scientific establishment, hierarchical SLAs can be set up. The hierarchy is created by identifying as many common elements as possible across SLAs, and negotiating these at as high a level as possible. This reduces the total number of negotiations, and their scope. The process can be simplified further by using word processing technology to construct and store multiple SLAs with common elements.

Three levels of hierarchy are usually enough, before the complications outweigh the benefits.

At the top level, parameters will apply to all services. These can probably be signed off with one signature at a level of control shared by both IT and the business area. For example, the highest level parameters for SLAs between IT and multiple business sites would be signed off by a senior manager whose responsibilities included both the business sites and IT.

At the next level, services common to a wide range of business users – perhaps in a particular division or one site of a multi-site operation – would be agreed either at a management level responsible for all users, or if necessary in collective negotiation with representatives of all the management areas involved. The services agreed here would constrain all subordinate SLAs.

At the bottom level, SLAs embodying or referring to the higher level clauses would be negotiated with individual groups of users or even, exceptionally, with individuals.

Negotiating Service Levels

Village-type relationships can cause particular problems for negotiating service levels within small units. The formality required can be undermined because:

- each side knows (or believes it knows) the other side's requirements
- personalities are well known
- bargaining positions have been the subject of extensive informal communication.

To counteract this, it is especially important that everyone in the IT unit understands about service level management (SLM), what it is for and how it works. They will all, consciously or not, be passing messages to customers.

The person responsible for fronting negotiations with customers is particularly important, since the credibility of service level management will start with the credibility and reputation of that individual. To succeed negotiators must have:

- *the respect of the IT unit* – otherwise they will not be able to establish what level of service can be offered in the negotiations
- *authority* – negotiators must be senior enough to be taken seriously and for their decisions to be acted upon. Usually this is determined by grading and pay levels
- *the respect of the IT unit's customers.*

6 Specialist software tools

Suitable software support tools are essential for IT Service management to operate effectively. Small IT units in particular have to rely on software tools to compensate for their lack of individual specialisms.

6.1 Software tools for SITUs

Tools for a small IT unit have substantively the same functionality as tools for larger units. This means that smaller units have to allocate a larger proportion of their budgets to pay for them. The higher cost can sometimes be balanced against what will probably be lower costs for storing a smaller number of configuration items. However, the number of CI *types* and *relationships* between CI types will not necessarily be less than for a larger unit. Indeed within certain types of organisation, for example scientific establishments, it will be higher, and may need extra processing power.

Technology can contribute significantly in a number of ways:

- *E-mail* – this can be used for submitting incidents and RFCs, and for sending service information to users
- *Telephony* – this includes techniques such as ACD (Automated Call Distribution), call queuing, 'intelligent' recorded messages, and of CTI (Computer Telephony Integration).

Further details on selecting tools are to be found in the CCTA Appraisal and Evaluation Guides.

The requirements for software support tools will need to cover:

- service support
- service delivery
- CAST (Computer Aided Software Testing) – regression testing, documentation and repeatability
- decision support.

6.1.1 Service Support

Greater change role
The combination of configuration management, change control and software control & distribution

Software to support the *greater change* function must be an integrated tool, with a consistent interface and a relational (or object-based) Database Management System (DBMS) to hold the common data. Because of the diversity and number of people who can access the data, it is important to have good networking capabilities and access control facilities.

Ideally, the Help Desk/incident logging/problem management tool should be based on the same technology as the tool for the greater change function. In particular, it should have a similar user interface, and either share a common database or relate to it through a simple data interchange. And again because of the need for wide access, the Help Desk tool must be networked and have excellent, flexible access controls.

6.1.2 Service Delivery

Requirements for availability management tools can often be put together from the detailed data kept by the service support tools, with in addition a further requirement for a simple predictive modelling component via a link to a spreadsheet.

As most aspects of capacity management, costing and contingency planning are probably going to be outsourced, tools which do more than collect data about the system's performance and usage may not be needed in-house. If these functions are retained in-house, the specialists involved will know what software support is appropriate

For a small ITSM team, automatic monitoring of critical service level agreement clauses is crucial. Tools must have good links to the low-level monitoring software – meaning that costing data can also be collected. And the Help Desk must have access to all the service level agreements held on the SLM support system, ideally via the Help Desk tool.

Artificial intelligence will make it possible to have high levels of automated support for incident and problem management, particularly for the intelligent screening of problem, known error and RFC databases.

6.1.3 CAST – regression testing, documentation and repeatability

Tools to support the testing of IT services are improving rapidly in the facilities, speed and features they offer. Two aspects of CAST are relevant to ITSM:

- *have the developers made use of testing tools?* – results must be available; suppliers, in-house or external, must be able to demonstrate that they have tested the new or revised software product adequately. Otherwise ITSM may wish to consider whether it will even accept the service for acceptance or operational testing

- *are there tools to assist in the areas of testing which come under ITSM's remit, ie acceptance and operational testing?*

Tools which assist in the running of tests can be attractive to small IT units because, once the initial investment has been made, they offer:

- a high degree of test coverage for a relatively small additional investment in staff time
- the ability to run tests automatically out of hours, reducing disruption to the service and the need for overtime.

They do, however, require maintaining to ensure the areas they test still reflect the users' requirements and to adapt to technical changes.

6.1.4 Decision support software

This term covers standard software tools such as spreadsheets and local database products. These are likely to be used by several of the ITSM functions. When buying these tools it is worth bearing in mind that:

- data and information from different sources within and outside ITSM will need to be merged and presented together. So the same spreadsheet and databases should be used as widely as possible, perhaps opting for the organisation standard (official or unofficial) rather than assessing all the options from scratch
- they will need to interface with any specialised support tools
- it is important for the ITSM's credibility to test the spreadsheets produced by users. It is all too easy to produce impressive-looking information which is not accurate.[7]

6.2 How to use tools successfully

Software tools aren't magic: they need careful selection, implementation and support before they work properly

Using software tools successfully is not just a question of buying them and loading them on to a hardware platform. Even in the smallest of units, introducing a software tool must be treated as a project which establishes the need for the tool, justifies its acquisition and makes sure that the right resources are put into installing it.

The informal nature of small IT units makes it tempting to think that service management tools can be implemented quickly at

---

[7] see section 7.5.2

minimal cost. This is simply not true. There are some established maxims for introducing tools which apply to all kinds of support tools in all sizes of IT unit.

The cost of the tool is more than the tool costs

Costs to consider after the initial investment include:

- preparing data for take-on
- staff training and familiarisation. In addition to basic training staff will need practice before they are competent
- developing and implementing any revised processes that the tool either requires or permits.

Introducing a new function will not save money

A new, comprehensive service management tool will make possible new processes and new information. This may improve services to customers. However, in the short term at least, introducing new functions will need extra time and money.

Automated chaos is just faster chaos

Before installing a tool, it is always worth spending time to try to improve current practices. For example, if configuration inventory figures are inaccurate, a state-of-the-art Configuration Management database will just provide a very detailed record of items that don't exist.

Beware the Silver Bullet lifecycle

No tool is a silver bullet, solving every problem at a stroke: it will take time before savings and improvements start to show.

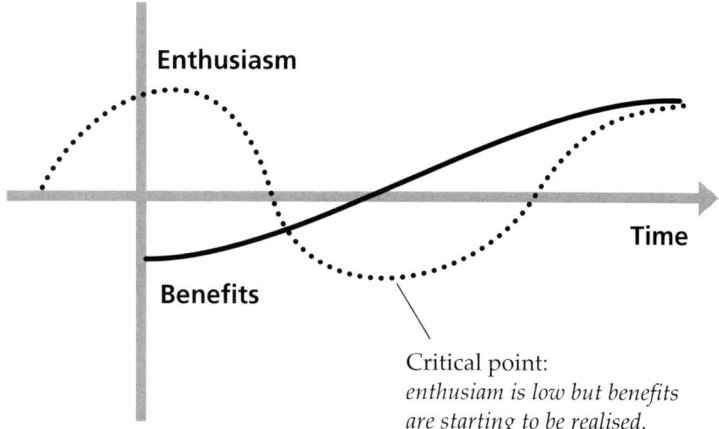

Critical point: *enthusiam is low but benefits are starting to be realised.*

Figure 11: Enthusiasm for a software tool may be at its lowest point just as the benefits are being realised.

This can affect people's enthusiasm for the new tool. Initially, they are keen but when learning difficulties and teething troubles appear, this enthusiasm will wane. At this point, there is a real danger of disillusionment killing off the tool, committing the organisation to a new round of problems and eventual disillusionment the next time. Management have a key role to play at this point, encouraging staff to persevere to the stage where, with familiarity, the tool becomes easy to use, and starts to produce the benefits that were promised.

One small IT unit installed a service support tool without realising the amount of staff time that would be needed, and the degree of management involvement for making decisions. Consequently the installation was rushed, and wrong (or worse still, no) decisions were taken at crucial moments. The result was a tool that did not support incident and problem management. Links to the data were inadequate and the base data was suspect and out of date. People working on the Help Desk felt cheated and unhappy. When last heard from, the organisation was replacing the tool in question with a new one. But no plans had been made to make extra resources available for taking it on and making it work.

And so the cycle repeats itself. At least this time the Help Desk staff did not expect so much . . .

Also under this heading comes the warning not to believe everything sales staff promise. If the organisation's level of technical knowledge is a problem, a third party should be brought in, either from elsewhere in the organisation, from a consultancy or from another organisation that already has the tool or a different one.

6.2.1 Justifying tools

The smaller the organisation, the higher a percentage of the budget a support tool is likely to be. This makes it harder for small units to justify tools, and especially to justify an integrated service management tool, rather than one which does a part of the job only. Even so, even the smallest of units will probably still benefit from using an integrated service support tool, because:

- by combining many functions in a single tool, the tool should provide:
  - a cheaper option in the long run than several different tools
  - a single learning curve, allowing savings to accrue more quickly
  - an integrated picture of incidents and errors, allowing Help Desk staff to resolve more incidents without escalation
- the procedures established will minimise dependence on one or two individuals
- holding information electronically rather than on paper is much safer and cheaper, with important implications for contingency and back-up. Copying an electronic database many times is trivial; copying a paper data bank is almost impossible.

6.3 User guides

Up-to-date and user-friendly guides can provide valuable support for IT staff

If user guides are simple to follow, a well-presented and up-to-date handbook can greatly ease the day-to-day burden falling upon small ITSM sections. At their best, these documents can:

- reduce the number of trivial incidents caused by users not understanding their systems and reporting as incidents simple things they could fix themselves, such as switching equipment on, resetting systems or even waiting long enough for things to happen
- encourage people to use services more widely by explaining what they are, what they can and can't do and how to access them

- encourage people to follow procedures, especially requests for change, by laying them out clearly and either providing appropriate forms or describing the electronic logging process
- provide a single point for all the IT information needed at users' workstations, including information for third-party repairers such as settings and options for equipment.

But if documents are difficult to understand, incomplete, wrong or out-of-date (as they unfortunately are in many organisations) they merely compound the problems they are designed to solve.

To make sure documents provide real and valuable benefits, it is worth following some simple rules:

- *ensure someone is responsible for the accuracy of the documentation* – this should be a high priority role for SLM and/or Help Desk. The change control process must include changes to the handbook as part of any change to IT services
- *allocate resources to maintaining documentation properly* – if money and resources are not budgeted for, all the time, effort and money spent on developing the guide in the first place will be wasted
- *involve users in creating and maintaining the documentation* – business sections can include help and advice on the procedures specific to their work and/or location
- *test the documents* – testing should be both from an IT point of view, for technical accuracy, and from the users' perspective, for accuracy in the work context and for usability
- *publicise the documentation to customers* – customers should know what is in it and how to use it. It must look and sound easy to use. One approach is to use friendly names to help keep guides in users' minds, such as
    - HINTS *Handbook for INformation Technology Services* (courtesy of ODA)
    - LITES *Local IT Equipment and Services manual*
- *make sure ITSM staff are familiar with it* – they are then likely to refer users to it for guidance

- *control copies* – each copy should be a controlled item under the configuration management or asset control system. Asset audits should check that it is:
  - where it is expected to be. If not, it is worth checking the reason. Perhaps it has been moved to somewhere more useful
  - up to date
  - well-used, thumbed and ragged. If not, the number and type of incidents logged from that location should be checked.

For an electronic handbook, it is also important to realise that:

- many users will print it out, preferring to read paper rather than screens. So it is easy for users to be referring to out-of-date documents
- if the system goes down, so does the handbook!

7 Processes on the fringe of ITSM

Within a large IT unit, there will be several independent divisions. As the picture is scaled down, fewer people mean that the number of divisions will also reduce.

Tasks which are independent in a larger organisation must fit into whatever divisions the small unit provides. Tasks which generally provide a service to customers are best placed under the IT Services Management umbrella.

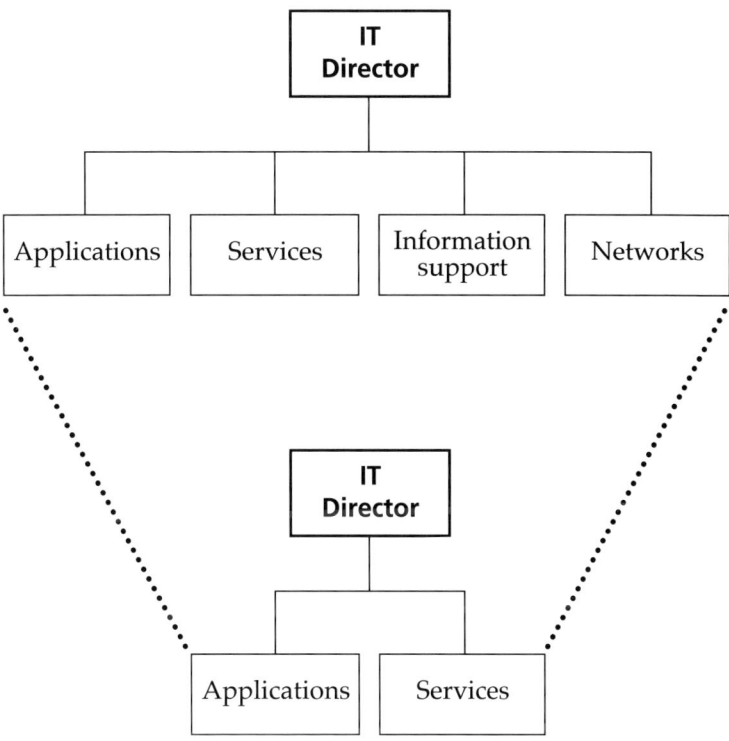

Figure 12: the shrinking organisation

7.1 System Security

The IT unit has a real responsibility to safeguard customers' data

IT managers are responsible for safeguarding customers' data while that data is within their domain. Since virtually all IT environments are subject to one or more threats to data, equipment or facilities, this is an important responsibility, and managers must use their limited resources to provide the most appropriate protection possible. In addition, if data is subject to the Data Protection Act, there is a requirement to make every effort to protect all personnel data. This means putting in place appropriate IT, procedural and physical security controls.

7.1.1 Security Risk Analysis

Security Risk Analysis provides a way of identifying threats, vulnerabilities and risks to systems, staff and facilities. Each risk is assessed, often in terms of historical or actuarial data, so that its impact can be costed. Then a range of measures to counter the threats can be planned and costed, and cost benefit recommendations drawn up. Depending on the budget available, and the level of risk that is acceptable, a selection of measures can be introduced.

Unless there are experienced security staff in the unit, the initial security assessment should be done by an external consultant with a proven track record in this field. Tools such as CRAMM (CCTA Risk Assessment and Management Method) capture many years of security best practice to help professionals with such assessments, but despite some claims to the contrary they will not replace expertise. Using untrained staff is counter-productive, lulling the IT manager into a false sense of security.

7.1.2 Detecting Viruses

Virus
In this context a virus is any unwanted software which can infiltrate into an IT system. Many viruses have detrimental, effects upon the systems they infiltrate

A 1994 DTI survey revealed that over 80% of the organisations who responded had experienced a virus attack within the previous twelve months. Some viruses are relatively benign, but others cause significant disruption. For most organisations the worst kind are those which cause minor data corruption over a long period of time, thus also corrupting back-up copies.

Organisations which exchange media, such as scientific research centres, are particularly prone to attack and accidental infection. Appropriate defence techniques include:

- *screening all incoming media* – everything should be loaded on to a standalone machine dedicated to virus detection
- *installing virus detection software* – this software runs in the background on each PC and system processor, checking continually. But it can slow down system performance
- *firewall devices* – communication links with the outside world (for example, the Internet) are mediated by devices which prevent unauthorised access to the network
- *raising awareness* – this means constantly reinforcing staff and users' awareness of both the risks and the virus protection measures in place
- *holding regular software audits* – these will identify unauthorised software
- *holding master software in quarantine* – this ensures it cannot become infected. Software Control and Distribution can hold it in the Definitive Software Library.

ITSM Virus checking service

In support of the organisation's virus detection policy ITSM must offer a service that is fast, easy and user-friendly.

If it is perceived as not being all of these, it will not be used, representing the worst of all worlds since you will have all the disadvantages of a virus protection system with no benefits:

- the expense of virus protection
- performance constraints on the system
- administrative and training overheads for staff

    but

- inadequate protection.

It is worth considering *anything* which might make virus screening easier and so more widely used. Draconian threats and punishments for those who bypass the protection will not work – they merely provide a scapegoat if things go wrong, which is no help at all to a business crippled by loss of data or operational facilities. Ways of improving co-operation might include:

- a no-blame policy to encourage staff to raise the alarm at the earliest sign of a possible infection
- taking the service to users, using a portable PC

- making sure that any games software is authorised as virus free. Many organisations ban all games to prevent viruses, but others find this merely encourages their illicit introduction
- checking how effective protection is, possibly by:
  - seeding benign viruses
  - holding software audits
  - carrying out anonymous surveys.

The user-friendliness of the service ITSM provides will depend upon many factors including:

- the perceived risk of infection
- the amount of predicted damage caused by infection
- the independence of users
- the common sense of users – there is no reliable link between users' common sense and their intelligence, IT awareness or grade.

ITSM is providing a service for the protection of the whole organisation, and any shortcuts or penny pinching could prove expensive if things go wrong. On the other hand, if the service is not universally used, then it is probably a waste of money.

7.2 Business Continuity Management

Business Continuity management goes beyond contingency planning to look at all the factors that need to be protected if the business is to survive – not just IT

Business Continuity Management (BCM) is about making sure that organisations can continue to operate after a disaster. BCM involves:

- identifying the business processes which need protection
- identifying cost-effective ways of reducing risks to the processes
- identifying key support functions for each process
- working out how to provide that support in any foreseeable disaster scenario.

IT contingency planning is concerned with how to maintain a basic level of IT support for the business in the event of a disaster. The ITIL module on contingency planning describes in detail the various options for ensuring continuity.

But while it is essential to preserve IT services if a business is to survive a disaster, it is not enough. There are many examples of organisations failing to survive in spite of a heavy investment in IT contingency, simply because they ignored other much more modest precautions to ensure business continuity. Especially in a small organisation, the IT unit can take the lead on business continuity, since their own plans are likely to be more developed than those of any other operational or support area.

On more than one occasion the IT services manager has been responsible for triggering the introduction of BCM within an organisation. A good example is the submission of an ITSM contingency plan to the managing director. The plan was accompanied by a note from the IT services manager

This note explained that she understood the commercial significance of the organisation's disaster recovery plans, and the need for confidentiality. She realised this was why she did not have access to them. It was essential though that the ITSM plans fitted in with the organisation's plans as a whole. Could the MD (who would of course be privy to the full disaster recovery plans) therefore confirm that the ITSM contingency plans as submitted were consistent with those of the whole company?

Within a week the IT Service Manager was responsible for managing a feasibility study on BCM for the organisation.

Guidance on BCM is available as part of ITIL.

7.3 Data management

It makes sense for ITSM to be closely involved with data management throughout the business

ITSM is likely to be closely involved with many aspects of data management. This involvement includes:

- *acting as data steward* – this means being responsible for administrating and promoting changes to data definitions
- *providing administration for databases* – ITSM can be responsible for the day-to-day administration of any Database Management Systems (DBMS).

Regarding data as part of the IT infrastructure, and therefore as part of ITSM's responsibility, has many advantages. These include:

- improved change impact analysis
- improved capacity management
- more attention given to data availability and contingency issues
- seeing data as a corporate resource[8].

---

[8] See CCTA's Information Management Library volumes on Data Management for further detail (see bibliography).

Dangers inherent in including Data Management in ITSM's responsibilities include:

- underestimating the strategic importance of Data Management
- over-dependence on the DBMS software.

7.4 Software maintenance

Software maintenance may be better placed with systems developers

In all IT units, strong links exist between problem management and software maintenance. In a small unit, software maintenance is likely to be a part-time or even an ad-hoc role for systems developers. The unit may choose to place the entire responsibility for managing software incidents with the application development staff.

7.5 Testing and acceptance of hardware and software

Testing can be done by outsiders, but users need to be involved if they are to understand and support their system

Small IT units are not likely to develop specialist independent testing sections. Testing applications which have been developed in-house can be done by cross-team testing within the development section. ITSM will be involved in:

- *operational testing* – this is appropriate since ITSM will operate the systems when they are part of the live service
- *load and capacity testing* – this ensures that there is enough capacity available to support the new or revised service
- *acceptance testing of hardware* – this should be done before it is connected to the live service.

In a small IT unit ITSM are in a particularly good position to ensure that all the components of an IT service operate together, and to work with users on the acceptance testing of a system.

It is possible to outsource such testing, but units will have to balance the advantages of this against the awareness that their own staff and customers will be using the system for years to come. If they are involved in acceptance testing, they are likely to be happy and supportive of the system when it goes live.

7.5.1 Business testing

However carefully the component parts of a business process have been tested, what really matters is how well everything works together. This has given rise to the belief that the only real test is live running – that the proof of the pudding is in the eating. But while ultimately this must be true, it is often possible to test the whole process before live running. This kind of business testing is likely to be a more cost-effective and practical proposition in a small organisation, with simpler logistics and more co-operative staff.

Case example

A turnkey system has been procured to convert paper records to microfiche for archiving. The system must process 3 A4 sheets per minute. An acceptance test of the IT hardware and software might be whether the equipment can convert one sheet in 20 seconds. But to the business what matters is that this rate can be achieved over a day or week in normal working conditions; that 6660 sheets go through the door marked IN, and after a week, the same number of microfiche records emerge from the door marked OUT. In addition, these sheets must be identifiable and the data recoverable.

By considering the business requirement, it becomes evident that merely watching the conversion process won't answer the key question – will the service support the business in the way it needs?

7.5.2 Spreadsheets and personal databases

All too often spreadsheets and local databases are created by end-users and subjected to little if any testing. Although they qualify as software development and should follow the same rules as any other development, the rules are seldom applied. People seem to have total faith in figures that are produced by the computer, especially if they are presented in the sophisticated formats available from modern software products, and even if they have not been tested or verified. Since many important business decisions will probably be made from information in user-developed spreadsheets and databases, some protection is necessary. This might include:

- *providing training in testing spreadsheets* – this might even mean restricting access to trained users
- *raising awareness by telling horror stories* – senior managers can be told horror stories from their own organisation, about spreadsheets which weren't tested properly. If there are no horror stories, this is probably either because nobody uses spreadsheets, or the errors haven't been spotted yet
- *explaining the pitfalls of self-testing* – there are strong psychological reasons why it is impossible for writers of spreadsheets or databases (or indeed a piece of prose) to self-test and find their own errors
- *providing a testing service* – the IT unit tests user-developed spreadsheets itself.

ITSM staff themselves are likely to want to develop spreadsheets and databases for management information. They should not be too proud to take advice from application developers and testers in the IT unit.

Self-Testing
People have an unavoidable tendency to see what they expect to see. So self-testing does not find errors, since people do not see what may actually be there

8 Measuring performance

An IT unit's performance is judged by the quality of the service it provides to users, and on how well it can fulfil service level requirements.

A good level of performance depends not only on the ability of IT systems to support the user workload, but also on the efficiency of the ITSM team in making the most of them. Units should constantly think about how to improve their performance, questioning the professionalism of their interface with users, the effectiveness of their problem management system, their ability to manage risk and so on.

8.1 Objectives and metrics

Metrics can be very revealing, but only when the right things are measured

In order to improve performance, there must be some measure of what that performance is, against which improvements or otherwise can be judged. There are many measurable items in IT Service management; it makes sense for an organisation to:

- identify those which matter most to their situation
- measure the current performance
- set objectives for improvement
- monitor measures to see if objectives have been met.

If a few key metrics are identified correctly, monitoring can give management a good ongoing indication of the unit's performance in terms of delivering a quality IT service efficiently and effectively. However, as with all things, it costs time and money to produce and interpret measures. So as well as monitoring the metrics in terms of the unit's performance, it is important to monitor their relevance as measures. For a small unit, where the overheads of measurement can quickly become significant, it is worthwhile reducing the number of variables measured by identifying:

- *measures that vary together* – if different measures are not independent, it is probably only worth measuring one of them
- *expensive measures* – some measures are much more expensive to monitor than others
- *ambiguous measures* – these can be influenced by a number of different factors and are open to multiple interpretations

- *widely fluctuating measures* – except where they can be identified with obvious corresponding peaks and troughs.

Broadly speaking, there are two kinds of measures:

- *external* – these directly measure the scale or quality of the delivered service
- *internal* – these measure the internal processes underpinning the service.

Some measures can straddle this boundary and give indications of performance both above and below the waterline, such as the number of calls to the Help Desk.

Case example

The number of calls to the Help Desk is one of the most popular, and yet one of the hardest measures to interpret. It is a very popular measurement, primarily because it is very easy to collect. But it is very hard to interpret; since nobody rings the Help Desk because they want to but because they need to. Thus the measurement depends on other variables.

Possible reasons for an increase in calls can be manifold and contradictory. For example:

- a bad help desk might attract more calls, because users have to keep calling until their problem is resolved
- a good help desk might receive more calls because users, encouraged by a good service, are using it more often
- a new release or change of software will attract more calls
- any change of staff or working practices will result in more calls because users are not so familiar with the service
- the work may be seasonal, so that less familiar parts of the IT system are being used at certain times of the year
- there may be a problem with the delivery of the service, such as
  – changes not being properly tested
  – software getting out of step across a distributed system
  – network or hardware going down.

All this shows that metrics are not independent, and not easy to interpret; just because something is easy to count does not mean that it should become a key ITSM measurement.

8.1.1 External metrics

Measurements which directly affect customers' ability to use the IT service will appear within SLAs. Most small units would find it worthwhile measuring:

- availability of IT at the desk-top
- time between reporting an incident and being told it is resolved

- time the Help Desk takes to
  - respond to a caller and log an incident
  - resolve an incident (broken down by category and priority)
- time taken to process change requests, including
  - acknowledging an RFC
  - approving or rejecting an RFC
  - implementing approved changes, including the success rate.

These external measures relate directly to the service being delivered to the customer above the waterline.

There will also need to be measurements of the actual workload which fulfilling the SLAs implies – this is probably kept to an agreed limit in the SLAs.

8.1.2 Internal metrics

In order to deliver the required levels of service, there will be many underpinning, internal ITSM processes, which ITSM must measure and monitor to maintain its services. These metrics will not be directly relevant to the customer. They might include:

- availability of components, such as
  - networks
  - servers
  - software packages
  - communication and systems software
  - electricity
- breakdown of the time taken to fully repair each component, including:
  - recognising and recording the fault
  - maintainers' response
  - actually fixing components
  - restoring the system
  - informing customers
- Help Desk statistics, consisting of:
  - number of incidents solved at first level and number requiring escalation
  - time spent on each call
- contribution to the change process, measured by:
  - comments on RFCs from staff members
  - length and frequency of change meetings
  - number of changes requiring back-out and resubmitting

- errors found during testing and stages where they were discovered.

8.1.3 Measuring customer perceptions

All the measures described so far are hard – that is, they can be expressed as numbers. It is the way those numbers change over time, taken with the changes in workload and other external influences, that matter to ITSM mangers. But IT units should not forget that hard measures are not, by any means, the whole picture.

As American management guru Tom Peters observed:

> 'Perception is all there is... The man who said you can only manage what you can measure was probably a very good scientist – he certainly never ran a successful business.'

The mind-set of the typical IT professional is one which lends itself to absolute numeric measures of performance, so they expect to be judged that way. But the majority of business users are unlikely to think in the same way. They will be more interested in how the service feels. For example, one of the most quoted statistics for Help Desks is the number of times the telephone is not answered within four rings. This statistic has the attraction of being easy to collect. In practice what affects the customer's perception of the Help Desk is the first 10 seconds of conversation after the telephone is answered. The right words and attitudes then can produce instant forgiveness for that 5th ring. This is not, however, at all easy to measure.

Research on customer satisfaction and expectations in the airline industry shows that customer perceptions are principally affected by a few key moments of interaction with staff. These are fairly easy to spot for airlines – at the check-in desk, or boarding the plane. Applying this to the ITSM environment shows how vital the first few seconds of conversation between customer and Help Desk are.

Customers will judge a service by how much use it is to them in their work. They will be willing to forgive a surprising number of troubles, niggles and inadequacies if they perceive that IT systems, and support services for them, add value to their work.

Units should try always to establish what goes right, as well as where they fail to meet targets. Often this kind of added value goes unnoticed. It is the service above and beyond the call of duty that really impresses users; but it can be eclipsed and prevented by a culture too concerned with mundane everyday measures.

8.2 Health checks and assessments

It is always difficult for any organisation to really know how well it is doing its job. It is axiomatic that to provide comparison against the norms, or to see what is not being done, an external view is required. In IT this view usually comes from an external consultancy. In order to help the evaluation process, there are several methods and techniques available, including assessment methods, health check packages and structured questionnaires.

There are two public deliverables from a typical evaluation product:

- an assessment of current performance
- a plan for improvement.

8.2.1 Assessment of current performance

This may a number or chart which makes an arithmetic comparison with industry and/or sector norms. This assessment is probably mostly of marketing significance. It may also be relevant if the unit needs to demonstrate its competence against actual or potential rivals, for example in a market testing, Compulsory Competitive Testing or other outsourcing situation.

8.2.2 Plan for improvement

This details specific target areas for improvement and, ideally, measurable objectives. It is of far greater use to the working IT unit, because it shows how to concentrate limited resources in areas that will increase effectiveness and efficiency.

The quality of the improvement proposals depends on:

- management commitment to the exercise
- staff attitudes
- the skills of the individuals carrying out the exercise (the method used will help pinpoint the weak areas, but is unlikely to offer solutions tailored to your environment).

8.2.3 Implementing health checks

The consultant performing the health check must be familiar with best business practice in the areas being checked. However refined the method or questionnaire, this kind of exercise is at most 50% science, with the rest being more of an art, depending on knowledge, experience, skill in data-gathering and the ability to gain co-operation from staff who may initially be hostile and suspicious.

The effort involved in performance of a health check will vary depending upon the scope of the check and the size of unit. In general, however, a health check should take no more than twenty man days to complete, often significantly less. A comprehensive survey of an IT unit can be carried out by two consultants over a week, with perhaps up to 6 man days more to prepare, write up and present the findings. If more than twenty-five man days are being proposed, consider:

- *are any benefits identified likely to be outweighed by the cost of the check itself?*
- *can you cope with all the information and proposals that will be generated from this work?* – you will have limited resources, funds and time to take the improvement plans on board; especially management time to champion them.
- *is the proposal too wide ranging?* – perhaps it would be better to spend less at the start, to identify which areas would benefit from a more detailed look
- *what else could the money be spent on?* – running the unit comes first, improving it second.

Small units are likely to benefit from a more general view than large ones, where health checks of more limited scope are sensible. So it is much harder in the small unit to make sure the right survey is being carried out. Many of the methods in current favour are aimed at particular parts of the IT unit, for example software production, IT Service Management or security. All of these areas and methods have overlap. For a wide ranging view, the outside consultancy has to have expertise across the whole range of IT disciplines; ideally it can provide individuals experienced and qualified in assessments and health checks over more than one area. It could be sensible to spend one or two days of consultancy on a feasibility study which would explain the options, provide written evidence and justify any accurately targeted further spend.

9 Bibliography

IT Infrastructure Library books.

Naturally, most of the ITIL books will be relevant to anyone involved in delivering IT Services. Information on the content and scope of individual ITIL books can be obtained from ITIMF or the ITIL management organisation. (This will be CCTA until late 1995.) All ITIL books are published by HMSO and can be ordered either directly from HMSO or through ITIMF at £35 each.

IT Service Management

The ITIL Pocket Guide – designed as a handy reference book for ITIL practitioners, who already know ITIL terminology
ISBN 0-9524706-0-8.

Published by ITIMF, Norwich; £9.95 (discounts for members and multiple copies).

Data Management

A series of three CCTA books on Data Management:
Data Management ISBN 0-11-330643-2
Corporate Data Modelling ISBN 0-11-330614-8
Data Management Standards ISBN 0-11-330670-9

All published by HMSO and available via ITIMF at £35 each.

Strategic Planning

Strategic Planning for Information Systems ISBN 0 471 92522 5

Published by John Wiley & Sons.

Annex A
Glossary of terms

A.1 Acronyms

BCS	British Computer Society
CAST	Computer Aided Software Testing
CI	Configuration Item
DSL	Definitive Software Library
IDPM	Institute of Data Processing Managers
IS	Information Systems
IT	Information Technology
ITIMF	IT Infrastructure Management Forum
ITSM	IT Service Management
LSA	Local Systems Administrator
PC	Personal Computer
RFC	Request For Change
SDM	Structured Design Method
SITU	Small IT Unit
SLA	Service Level Agreement
SSADM	Structured Systems Analysis and Design Method
TQM	Total Quality Management

A.2 Definitions of terms

Configuration Item

A component of an IT infrastructure – or an item, such as a request for change, associated with an IT infrastructure which is (or is to be) under the control of configuration management.

Definitive Software Library

A library where all quality-controlled versions of all software configuration items are held in their definitive form.

Greater Change Role

The combination into one work role of Configuration Management, Change Control and Software Control & Distribution.

ISO9000

The International Standards Organisation series of standards relating to Quality Management.

IT Infrastructure

An organisation's computers and networks – hardware, software and computer-related telecommunications, upon which application systems are built and run.

IT Infrastructure Management Forum

The Independent Management Forum for Users of CCTA's IT Infrastructure Library.

Local Systems Administrator

The person responsible for the day-to-day control of IT equipment, and the services running on that equipment, sited within the customer domain. The Local Systems Administrator will usually be a member of the business community, looking to the IT directorate for technical support.

Annex B
IT Service Management – task allocation guide

B.1 Introduction

Section 5.1 discusses the options available to an IT unit for meeting IT Service Management task requirements. Five options were identified and explained briefly. This annex repeats and expands those options and then offers a breakdown of the ITSM tasks, indicating the possible sourcing of each task against the five identified options. This annex is written on the assumption that a decision has been made to retain an in-house IT Services function.

B.1.2 Breakdown of possible sourcing of ITSM functions

The five categories identified and used throughout this annex are as follows.

ITSM provides

These tasks need to be retained and performed by an in-house IT Services section. They fall into two broad categories:

- roles that interface directly with the customer and user, such as the day-to-day Help Desk – user communications, negotiating and agreeing service levels and initial consideration of change requests
- monitoring and controlling the underpinning ITSM functions.

ITSM jointly provides

These tasks can be performed by IT services in partnership with another provider (this may be third-party or in-house application development or business units). The identity of the suggested partner(s) can be found in the grid below. Much of any necessary initiation work will be a partnership between external consultants and in-house staff.

Business provides

Best supplied by staff within the business function (although the cost may still be seen as part of supporting IT within the organisation). This approach is recommended for tasks such as:

- defining the aims of the IT Service Management function
- contingency (and business continuity) for IT equipment under the day-to-day control of users
- local filtering of incidents and day-to-day operation of locally sited equipment (Local Systems Administrators).

Third party provides

Best outsourced to external experts/service providers. Mostly these are tasks requiring specialist knowledge and skills. Such skills are required for only a small percentage of the time and it is thus not economically viable to recruit and/or train in-house staff with those skills. Indeed the range of such knowledge across the ITSM functions would make it impossible to provide all these tasks using in-house staff in anything less than a middle sized IT unit. The other major area of third-party input is in the establishment of new or changed procedures and requirements. This type of work is especially suited to third-party supply since:

- by its very nature it is additional work, over and above the current tasks of supporting customers, and thus the introduction of additional resources to meet it is logical
- it is an area where previous experience is beneficial, again this experience must come from outside the unit, either from a third party or new staff
- an external view may be more objective and less influenced by current and historical practice.

Developer provides

Supplied by the application development and/or maintenance staff, covering functions that:

- require applications expertise and experience, such as enhancing, modifying and testing software support tools
- define and establish ITSM parameters within new and changed applications, such as capacity and availability requirements
- manage problems, especially in correcting software faults or preventing software-related incidents.

B.2 Caveats

This Annex has been developed against a general concept of a small IT unit's IT Service Management needs; it cannot be prescriptive nor apply to all possible circumstances. In particular the picture will be modified (heavily in some instances) by the following influences:

- the particular skills and experience that happen to be available from the staff currently working in
  - IT Services
  - application development
  - business communities
- consultancy services available (either independent or perhaps within a parent organisation's IT directorate)
- financial constraints; it costs money to hire consultants, new staff, to retrain existing staff or to do new things. The need to balance requirements and funds is one well known and understood by managers everywhere
- existing strengths and weaknesses in the current ITSM offerings
- perceived needs of the customer base.

B.3 Task by task breakdown of possible sourcing for ITSM

The tables following indicate suggested sourcing for:

- generic tasks, those needed to introduce the ITIL approach and those concerned with planning, implementing, monitoring and controlling that are common to all (or many) of the individual functions
- the tasks specific to the individual 'core' ITIL functions (ie those within the service support and service delivery sets, as covered by the ITIL Pocket Guide).

It is important to recognise that retaining a task in-house does not mean that other parties will not be involved via consultation and normal customer/supplier relations. Conversely, the 'off-loading' of a task outwith ITSM will not absolve ITSM of appropriate involvement, but that control and responsibility for the tasks has been passed over.

B.3.1 Generic ITSM tasks

	ITSM provides	ITSM jointly provides	Business provides	Third party provides	Developer provides
Tasks in role definition					
defining the mission statement for the IT service		✔	✔	✔	
setting aims and objectives for the IT service		✔	✔	✔	
Tasks in awareness raising					
communicating the benefits of the IT service	✔			✔	
circulating information through seminars, meetings, leaflets or circulars	✔			✔	
Tasks in planning					
producing a statement of requirements for the specified ITIL functions	✔			✔	
defining detailed requirements				✔	
quantifying the workload of the new service	✔			✔	
producing guidelines about how the service will work – its structure and relationship to the organisational structure	✔			✔	
specifying target performance measurements	✔		✔	✔	
designing the process the function is to perform, including support for it	✔			✔	
producing an implementation plan	✔			✔	
defining ITSM staff training requirements	✔			✔	
describing benefits, costs and possible problems	✔		✔	✔	

B.3.1 Generic ITSM tasks *continued*

	ITSM provides	ITSM jointly provides	Business provides	Third party provides	De-veloper provide
Tasks in implementation					
developing and validating the process	✔			✔	
installing software and equipment	✔			✔	
customising packaged computer tools				✔	✔
testing the process	✔		✔		✔
creating inventories for software and equipment	✔			✔	
writing support documents	✔			✔	
training staff	✔			✔	
carrying out acceptance testing	✔		✔		
going live	✔				
Tasks in post-implementation review and audit					
reconciling requirements with reality – checking that services are providing what users want		✔		✔	
comparing actual activity levels with forecasts		✔		✔	
assessing how staff feel about the service		✔		✔	
reviewing effectiveness and efficiency		✔		✔	
identifying benefits			✔	✔	
reviewing the management of the project		✔		✔	
preparing review reports		✔		✔	
carrying out regular audits				✔	
monitoring, reviewing and fine-tuning how effective the service is	✔				

B.3.1 Generic ITSM tasks *continued*

	ITSM provides	ITSM jointly provides	Business provides	Third party provides	Developer provides
Tasks in supporting the development cycle					
make sure that requirements for running and maintaining systems are taken into account from the start					✔
create testing strategies for IT services	✔				✔
assess the impact of new or changed systems on the existing IT infrastructure and services	✔				
understand from the start what everyone will need from the system	✔				✔
Tasks in achieving customer focus					
advising and helping IT customers to make the best use of IT services		✔	✔		
passing on customers' views and ensuring comments are acted on		✔	✔		
following up customers' complaints	✔				
monitoring how customers perceive the quality of their IT services		✔	✔		
encouraging internal user groups			✔		
initiating customer care programmes	✔				
making sure that properly trained Help Desk staff are available	✔				
providing feedback to staff		✔	✔		
tracking the customers' business needs to ensure IT services continue to meet them		✔	✔		

B.3.2 Help Desk

	ITSM provides	ITSM jointly provides	Business provides	Third party provides	Developer provides
Help Desk day-to-day tasks					
to provide a customer interface	✔		✔		
to manage the Incident Control system	✔				
as support for business operations			✔	✔	✔
to provide management information	✔				
to provide information to users (bulletins etc)		✔		✔	
Tasks in setting up a Help Desk					
assessing the volume of calls you'll need to process	✔		✔		
deciding on a centralised or distributed structure				✔	
investigating what type of call logging to use (the hardware, the software and the telephone system)				✔	
defining the procedures for customers to follow when calling the Help desk		✔	✔	✔	
laying down the procedures for Help Desk staff in dealing with enquiries	✔				
training for customers and help Desk staff		✔		✔	
deciding on use of scripts		✔		✔	

B.3.3 Problem management

	ITSM provides	ITSM jointly provides	Business provides	Third party provides	Developer provides
Problem management tasks in incident control					
provide second level support (after Help Desk) for diagnosing and resolving difficult or major incidents				✓	✓
acts as co-ordinator for other specialist support (possibly via the Help Desk)	✓				
Tasks in problem control					
identifying, diagnosing and recording the root causes of incidents, to stop problems from a single source recurring		✓		✓	✓
carrying out severity analysis and providing appropriate support	✓			✓	✓
identifying potential problems before they can cause disruption to IT services	✓			✓	✓
maintaining problems database		✓		✓	✓
Tasks in error control					
initiating RFC, to prevent problems from occurring	✓				
putting right known errors, under the control of change management		✓		✓	✓
maintaining known errors database		✓		✓	✓

B.3.4 Change management

	ITSM provides	ITSM jointly provides	Business provides	Third party provides	Developer provides
Tasks in setting up change management					
consider who to involve in the Change Advisory Board		✓		✓	
define special arrangements for urgent changes		✓	✓	✓	
Tasks in change management					
processing RFC		✓	✓		✓
change scheduling	✓				
change building				✓	✓
change recording		✓		✓	✓
implementation		✓		✓	✓

B.3.5 Configuration management

	ITSM provides	ITSM jointly provides	Business provides	Third party provides	Developer provides
Tasks in configuration identification					
deciding the scope of items to be controlled		✓		✓	
deciding the level of items to be controlled, keeping a balance between the availability of information and the resources you'll need to collect and maintain it		✓		✓	
defining a naming convention		✓		✓	
recording variants – similar CIs with slight differences		✓		✓	
recording all CIs, their attributes and the relationships between them in a Configuration Management Database (CMDB)		✓		✓	
Control: To achieve control, the record of CIs has to be agreed and frozen. Changes can only take place with the agreement of the appropriate authorities. All CIs must be brought under change control	✓				
Status accounting (recording and reporting the current and historical status of each CI, including:)					
recording all changes to CIs in the CMDB	✓				
producing periodic status reports listing current CIs and their status	✓				
Verification (reviewing or auditing process which makes sure that all CIs conform with their records in the CMDB)					
checking physical CIs against status reports, confirming location, owner, specification etc		✓	✓	✓	

B.3.6 Software control and distribution

	ITSM provides	ITSM jointly provides	Business provides	Third party provides	Developer provides
authorising the software release	✓				
defining the software release	✓				✓
controlling releases	✓				
maintaining the Definitive Software Library (DSL)	✓			✓	✓
bringing software into service		✓	✓		✓
Tasks in setting up software control and distribution:					
all new or changed software to be rigorously tested, where possible before live running				✓	✓
all software to be tested for compatibility with the rest of the organisation's IT infrastructure	✓			✓	

B.3.7 Service Level Management

	ITSM provides	ITSM jointly provides	Business provides	Third party provides	Developer provides
creating a Service Catalogue		✓	✓	✓	
identifying service level requirements		✓	✓		✓
negotiating Service Level Agreements	✓				
reviewing support services				✓	
setting accounting policies		✓	✓	✓	
monitoring and reviewing services	✓			✓	✓
reporting	✓				

B.3.8 Cost management

	ITSM provides	ITSM jointly provides	Business provides	Third party provides	Developer provides
General tasks					
establishing formal IT costing – knowing what the costs of providing IT services are		✓	✓	✓	
optionally, implementing charging – recovering costs from users		✓		✓	
Detailed tasks – planning annually					
costing – establishing the standard unit costs for each major IT service		✓		✓	
charging – establishing a pricing portfolio and a 'price list' for each item		✓		✓	
Operations (perhaps monthly)					
monitor expenditure and compare plans to actuals by cost unit	✓				
compile and issue invoices		✓		✓	

B.3.9 Capacity management

	ITSM provides	ITSM jointly provides	Business provides	Third party provides	De-veloper provides
creating the capacity management database		✓		✓	
producing reports		✓		✓	
producing capacity plans				✓	
monitoring performance					
managing resources	✓			✓	✓
managing demand		✓	✓		
Tasks in structuring the capacity management function					
deciding if mainframe, midrange, PC and network capacity can be managed together by the same person or group		✓		✓	
deciding if the capacity planning and performance monitoring elements should be split		✓		✓	

B.3.10 Availability management

	ITSM provides	ITSM jointly provides	Business provides	Third party provides	Developer provides
Managing reliability					
measuring the reliability of each part of the infrastructure	✓				
specifying the resilience built into the IT service		✓		✓	✓
agreeing the level of preventative maintenance		✓		✓	
Managing service availability					
keeping IT in operation (maintainability)	✓			✓	✓
managing serviceability	✓			✓	
Tasks in the availability planning process					
determine what availability requirements are	✓		✓		
design for availability		✓		✓	
produce the availability plan		✓		✓	
Tasks in the monitoring and reporting of availability					
collect availability data	✓				
maintain the availability database		✓		✓	
monitor how IT services comply to availability requirements in SLAs and how contractors comply to serviceability requirements	✓				
report achieved availability levels to Service Level Manager and other IT service managers	✓				

B.3.11 Contingency Planning

	ITSM provides	ITSM jointly provides	Business provides	Third party provides	Developer provides
understanding what options for disaster recovery are available and choosing the right one		✓	✓	✓	
Tasks in the contingency management process					
analysing the impact of a disaster on the business and what counter measures are justified (using CRAMM)				✓	
producing the contingency plan		✓	✓	✓	
regularly testing and reviewing the contingency plan		✓	✓	✓	

Annex C
Where to go for advice

Staff in small IT units often feel isolated; compared to larger units, they have fewer fellow IT professionals within their daily environment. (The benefit, of course, is that they are more likely to be in daily professional and social contact with non-IT staff helping to develop a wider and more balanced view of their role within the organisation.) There are sources of advice and comparison available. Some potential contacts are given here:

- *User groups* – the IT Infrastructure Management Forum (ITIMF) is the group for users of ITIL. They are a useful source of contacts and advice as well as being sellers of the ITIL books and organising seminars and an annual conference. At the time of writing, there are active ITIMF organisations in both the UK and the Netherlands, and plans for one in South Africa. Contacts are
    - for Benelux – Jan van Bon +31 50 85 11 11.
    - UK and rest of world – Mick Brown +44 1603 767181

- *Other IT units* – your problems are rarely unique. Similar IT units are likely to have encountered similar problems to yourself. Consult with more than one such unit. Identify elements of the approaches best suited to your own environment. Formulate an approach and discuss with these units. ITIMF (and, for UK government organisations, CCTA) can often make connections and contacts

- *Consultancy* – consider the use of external consultants. Once again, solicit recommendations from managers of other IT units

- *The professional IT organisations* – these provide relevant services including specialist interest and regional groups, where ideas can be exchanged and mutual encouragement and problem sharing is encouraged. UK organisations are
    - IDPM, IDPM House, Edgington Way, Ruxley Corner, Sidcup, Kent DA14 5HR (tel 0181 308 0747)
    - BCS, 1 Sanford Street, Swindon SN1 1HJ (tel 01793 417417)

- *Regulatory bodies* – information concerning specialist areas can often be obtained from Government or other regulatory organisations. Examples (within the UK) are
    - Civil Service Occupational Health Service (CSOHS)
    - Health and Safety Executive (HSE)

- *CCTA* provides advice to its customers (UK government and associated organisations) and has also initiated a forum specifically for small and medium sized IT units (COSMIC); information is available from CCTA on 01603 740740.

Annex D
Suggested contents for a user handbook

D.1 Introduction

What a user handbook contains will, like everything else mentioned in this book, depend on the organisation being considered. There may even be a need to produce different versions within a single organisation if there is a clearly differentiated customer base. The following suggested potential contents are offered as a guide.

D.2 Universal items

What services the IT unit supports

A catalogue of the services available to users, how to access them, what they provide in terms of business support.

Help and advice

This part of the handbook would cover:

- simple things that can (and should) be checked before turning elsewhere for help
- where and how to get help from, eg:
  - local systems administrators
  - Help Desk
- how to report problems, when services are available, the information to gather together first
- priority allocation practices, what the categories mean, what rights the users have in categorising, rights of appeal in case of disagreement.

Glossary of terms

While jargon should be avoided wherever possible, its use is inevitable. In a handbook, designed to be referred to many times, its total avoidance will make explanations overlong, the book difficult to refer to quickly when required and tedious to read on subsequent occasions. All jargon that is used must be defined in simple terms. One option, as used in this guidance, is to define the word near the text where it is used, as well as in a separate glossary.

The handbook is not an IT document, it is intended to support business users and will thus also contain jargon appropriate to whatever business is being supported. This jargon needs to be defined along with any IT jargon used. Concise and easy to understand definitions will aid new users, often those most in need of the IT handbook, who are likely to be unfamiliar with the business terms, as well as IT ones. The most difficult jargon of all to cope with is the specialised usage of what, elsewhere, would be a word of general meaning. A very common example is the use made of the word 'quality'.

> **RFC – Request for Change**
> A formal mechanism for requesting a change to procedures

Procedures relating to changes

This section would include:

- change requests: the format required, where to submit them, what does and what doesn't require formal RFCs and prior approval, time scales for approval or rejection and any appeals procedures
- urgent change procedures, especially authority to define a change as urgent and rules on what might constitute 'urgent'
- notification of changes to ITSM: how users will be informed of staff changes and moves, new phone numbers, contact points etc, minor moves of equipment (where permitted).

Security issues

This has two areas of coverage:

- protection of data, eg
  - control of passwords
  - measures in place to protect against viruses and hacking
  - procedures for backing up data and programs and for recovering back-up software
- legal aspects, such as
  - Data Protection Act implications, especially on local software applications
  - software licensing, and copyright.

D.3 Probable items for inclusion

Procurement of IT equipment

Where users have the authority to purchase IT equipment for use within their business areas, the handbook would be likely to contain sections on purchasing:

- hardware and software products which are recommended and/or supported by the IT unit. Products might include typical PC configurations and software packages suitable for different types of users and applications
- advice on selecting and buying which might range from a simple recommendation to use the IT unit for purchasing, to guidance on comparison and evaluating value for money over the whole lifetime of a product.

Beginner's guides to PCs and software

This section would reflect the customers and users which the IT unit supports. Its main purpose is to try and establish a baseline level of knowledge which the Help Desk can assume is possessed by callers.

Auditing

The need for co-operation in audits of hardware and software carried out by ITSM. This would cover ITSM's rights of access to data (could be significant if restricted data is processed); need to label all items, use of personal software on the organisation's IT equipment.

D.4 Possible items for inclusion

Depending on the organisation, anything of relevance can be included. As the handbook becomes more used and an automatic first place to look for help, other sections may wish to have material included, from fire alarm procedures to welfare services and cafeteria facilities. Balance the benefits against the drawbacks:

Benefits of combining with other sections

- wide coverage and content mean wide interest in keeping it up-to-date
- single source of reference is more likely to be kept handy and actually referred to
- economies of scale in production
- likelihood of spotting overlaps and/or inconsistencies between procedures established by different sections.

Drawbacks of combining with other sections

- handbook becomes too large and cumbersome to use
- too much in it allied to bad or non-existent indexing means you can't find the bit you want
- inevitable inconsistencies appear

- ownership becomes shared and results in intractable committees deciding on format, reviews and content. This
    - delays updates, making it more likely to be out-of-date
    - prevents innovative use of presentational techniques
    - is likely to result in a stodgy prose style, after everyone has added their comments to proposed content.

Possible ITSM content

ITSM content could cover a wide range:

- procedures for testing local spreadsheets and database products
- training courses available for users
- customer surveys
- complaints (and congratulatory) procedure
- revision history of software and hardware.

Annex E
Stable infrastructures within a small IT unit

This annex specifically addresses the secondary target audience outlined in section 1.2.

E.1 Characteristics

The stable infrastructure is likely to consist of well established IT systems supporting a static business need. General characteristics of this kind of ITSM section might include:

- opportunity for less rigour in change management, ie there will not be many changes, what changes there are will be likely to affect only a small percentage of the service
- most things that can have gone wrong, will have. Thus there is a large store of known workarounds to remaining problems and incidents
- workload and requirements are well known, capacity and availability are not likely to be high profile tasks
- SLAs should be relatively easy to introduce into a known and stable background, but with some caveats
    - familiarity breeds contempt, so quite possibly IT does not have a high reputation, since it is not dynamic, nor driving the organisation into new areas
    - traditionally IT will have been a free resource, taken for granted; raising the profile with SLAs may engender a new outlook, new requests for service and improvement, which may in turn place an impossible workload on to a small resource
    - IT (especially ITSM) are unlikely to be well placed politically to negotiate with the business areas
- staff who are used to a stable, safe and untroubled life could be reluctant to adopt new ideas. However, these ideas may be essential if the work is to remain in-house.

E.2 Mixed environments

Many small IT units will combine a stable element, quite possibly based on well established mainframe or mini hardware, with a more dynamic PC and/or UNIX network service. However the unit is organised, this mix can cause problems since:

- either a single structure will cover both areas, when staff will need to be somewhat schizophrenic in treating the two areas according to their need, viz:
    - since the newer services will have the bulk of incidents and change requests, knowledge of the older services may be lost, or at least staff will be unfamiliar and more prone to making mistakes
    - users of the older service may perceive themselves as second-class users, bringing resentment which could spread and threaten the IT unit's position
    - it is difficult to switch between services that require urgent responses and those which can be dealt with more leisurely
- or, on the other hand, if the unit is organised around the two types of service, different problems arise
    - staff working on the older services can feel they are working in a dead-end area, with reduced prospects and may leave, complain or work unenthusiastically
    - a destructive rivalry can arise between the two areas, which may feel they are competing for resources and management attention
    - the stable environment is likely to find itself relying on one or two individuals who have been there a long time, know the services, the hardware and the major customers and who don't need to document what they are doing. This can cause serious trouble when those individuals leave.

When an organisation is considering outsourcing parts of their business (especially when under pressure to do so, eg from government initiatives), the stable element of the IT infrastructure may well be seen as a prime candidate. This can cause real animosity between the two groups of staff, where one sees their future threatened; transfers between the two sections can then become very difficult and subject to political rather than operational considerations.

Printed in the United Kingdom for HMSO
Dd. 301052 8/95 C6